Praise for *Fro*

"It has been a source of great i... n the life of a respected academic... , a dynamic and gifted preacher and an outstanding minister, Grady Wilson Powell, Sr., whose impact upon the community has been immeasurable. As a pioneer, he was faced with challenges during his career and has conquered them in ways that were uniquely Grady Powell. He established new precedents as he swam against the proverbial tide and shattered those glass ceilings known as the status quo. Empowering others to be the best they can be; enhancing the dynamics of the Christian witness; and guiding churches to experience phenomenal programmatic growth will be a part of his rich legacy. His mantra throughout his life has been 'Let excellence characterize all facets of your life.' You will cherish reading about each phase of the life of this servant of God."

Lucille Murray Brown
Superintendent, Retired, Richmond Public Schools

"Many senior adults find it therapeutic to write their memoirs. We can be glad that the Reverend Grady Powell was prompted to do so, for I am confident that his book will be judged one of the best. He lets you look behind the scenes of a busy and beloved pastor whose generation has seen more changes than any preceding one. Everyone has a story, but the narrative of Grady's life is not to be missed, from his earliest days until now. He was a founding member of American Baptist Churches of the South, bringing both predominantly black and white congregations together into the national body."

Robert Seymour
Minister Emeritus
Binkley Memorial Baptist Church in Chapel Hill

"I have had the privilege of observing Reverend Grady Powell preach from the pulpit on several occasions, and I can honestly say that he is one of the greatest preachers I have ever heard. Drawing on his vast knowledge of the Bible, combined with the skills of the master storyteller, Dr. Powell has the rare ability to attract the undivided attention of his listeners and deliver a profound message at the same time. Dr. Powell's autobiography, *From Morning 'til Evening*, does the same for its readers. The book contains a powerful message about family, overcoming obstacles, taking chances, justice, and love equal to any of his greatest sermons. Anyone who reads will be moved and inspired by the story of a remarkable man and his time."

Charles F. Bryan, Jr.
President and CEO emeritus, Virginia Historical Society

From Morning 'til Evening

Best Wishes

[signature]

From Morning 'til Evening

The Autobiography of
Grady W. Powell, Sr.

By Grady W. Powell, Sr.

BELLE ISLE BOOKS
www.belleislebooks.com

ISBN 978-1-9399303-0-9
Library of Congress Control Number: 2014946852

Printed in the United States

"I Walk with the King" by James Rowe and B. D. Ackley (1915) reprinted by permission

Published by
BELLE ISLE BOOKS
www.belleislebooks.com

I dedicate this autobiography to my wonderful family whose constant love and continuous support have brought inestimable encouragement and deeper meaning to my life:

Mom and Dad – Herbert and Lillie Powell

Siblings – Mable, Hampton, Percy, Mercy, Charlie and Irene

Wife – Bertie Jeffress Powell

Children – Sandra (Albert), Dorthula (Harvey), Grady Jr. (Danette), Herbert, and Eric

Grandchildren – Harvey III and Grady III

TABLE OF CONTENTS

INTRODUCTION

This is the story of one man's life: his love of family, his professional journey, and his unbending relationship with God. God spoke to him at a very young age and convinced him to preach the gospel. He gave his trial sermon at the age of seventeen. *From Morning 'til Evening* is the autobiography of my father, Rev. Grady W. Powell, Sr.

The "morning" period of his life chronicles his childhood, his family, and surroundings in Brunswick County, Virginia, and describes those persons around him who influenced his path. As the years go by, he gracefully moves into the "afternoon" time frame and transports himself from the fields of Brunswick County to the city streets of Lynchburg, then Richmond, and finally settles down in Petersburg, Virginia, in 1961. It is during this period that he constructs the building blocks that are to be the foundation for his life. He becomes a husband to Bertie Jeffress from Pittsburgh, Pennsylvania, in what is truly a brief chance encounter. He becomes a father to five children and meets his professional destiny standing at the pulpits of Quioccasin Baptist Church in Richmond and Gillfield Baptist Church in Petersburg. The "evening" period of his life finds him "dancing with retirement" as he goes from one church to the next doing interim pastorates, and having the time of his life at a slower pace but with the same intensity of style. The "evening" time frame also gives him an oasis upon which he can reflect on the deeper meaning of God, the importance of family, and a more introspective approach to the church.

Anyone who reads this vivid and emotional story about my father will be able to say this: "There goes a man who loves God, his family, and the people he serves." Those are the "shining stars" in his life. Everything else takes the status of "co-star."

What a joy it has been for me to participate with my father in putting together this story. We hope you will enjoy it! Let us begin . . .

Grady W. Powell, Jr.

I Walk with the King

By James Rowe & B. D. Ackley

In sorrow I wandered, my spirit oppressed,
but now I am happy, securely I rest.
From morning 'til evening, glad carols I sing,
and this is the reason,
I walk with the King.

I walk with the King, hal-le-lu-jah!
I walk with the King, praise his name!
No longer I roam, my soul faces home,
I walk and I talk with the King.

PART I
Early Morning

CHAPTER ONE

Birth and Growing Up in Ante

No bells rang; nor was there any country gathering, as is often done for important rural events; nor was there a grand announcement on Thursday, August 6, 1932, in the community of Ante, Brunswick County, Virginia. It was simply that another child was born to the family of Herbert Vermont Powell and Sallie Lillie Taylor Powell. Mom and Dad were not excited, because there had been six births already: two girls and four boys. Mable was ten; Hampton (we called him "Buster") was eight; Percy was seven; Mercy was six; Charlie (we called him "Toot") was four; and Irene was eighteen months. In ten years, seven children were born to this family. No, there were no grand celebrations. I understand why. I was told by Mom that there was excitement from the siblings. Irene wanted to hold the baby but was too young to be trusted. The pleasure would go to Charlie, "Toot," who was four. Generally my siblings were happy and excited to see an infant and to have a baby brother.

Naming me was a struggle. I would ask Mom many times how she arrived at the name Grady Wilson. I really wanted some good story that would give me talking points. Why was I not named James, after my paternal grandfather? Or Charles, after my maternal grandfather? Or Anthony, after my great-great-maternal grandfather? I would from time to time ask again and again. From my understanding of her oral history, there were many reasons. The strongest seemed to be slavery. For example, Great Grandpa Ant'ny was three generations from me. He was fathered by a plantation owner; while generally known, his parentage wasn't talked about.

How then did Mom arrive at the name "Grady Wilson"? It was the sawmill story. Often men who worked at traveling sawmills moved from place to place following that line of work. There was one sawmill worker whose name was Grady Wilson. Thus, my name. Aunt Sallie Ellis, who was the midwife, spelled it incorrectly. I did not learn this until I applied for a passport. I discovered at the Bureau of Vital Statistics that my name was Grady Wilson but it was spelled Graddie, and it remained that way until the seventies, when I got my passport under my proper name.

As I reflect on the births of the Powell children, and other familiar circumstances, I now understand why there was no great familial celebration. Mom was tired. The house was crowded and times were not easy. It was the height of the depression. Many times Mom told me of working in the tobacco fields the morning of my birth. Just before noon, she felt labor pains and left the field for the house. Daddy went by mule to get Aunt Sallie Ellis, the community midwife. Mable, my ten-year-old sister, was told to go to Aunt Pink's house. Yes, that was her name: Pink Eunice Pair. She was my dad's sister. At the time of my birth, she had ten children. One, Wilbert, was four months old when I was born. This little baby, "Samp," as we called him, would become my best friend, my buddy, and my confidant. We were inseparable from the time I knew anybody until we completed our high school education, graduating in the class of 1950 from Saint Paul's High School.

There was a special reason for sending Mable to Aunt Pink's house: because every birth occurred at home. The tradition was to send children to a trusted friend's home until the process of delivery was completed. Further, Aunt Pink would provide her meals and the children would play and enjoy one another during this waiting period. It worked well.

Aunt Sallie Ellis the midwife came. Mom and Sallie Ellis estimated her arrival time to be around 1:30 P.M. She had to estimate the time because the family had no mechanical timepiece—no watch and no clock. How could time be kept? By the position of the sun, the length of one's shadow, and one's internal clock. At about 3:30 P.M., August 6, 1932, I was delivered in Brunswick County, Virginia, two hours after Aunt Sallie arrived in my home.

The days of early childhood moved on in an uneventful fashion. The year was now 1938. I was six years old and it was time for me to go to elementary school. The name of that one-room school was Westwood Ford. My earliest recollection of going to Westwood Ford was that my sister Mable had to take me to be inoculated. What those shots were for I really don't know, but we called them "getting your shots for school." The school was located about three miles from my home and I remember Mable walking rather fast—really too fast for me. I was rather nervous about getting the shots. I had already decided, however, that I wasn't going to cry.

We finally walked around a bend, and a few hundred feet up the road was that one-room school. It was white. It had four to six windows on the north side and no windows on the south side. When we arrived, there were only a few people there.

Junior Taylor was the first one to get a shot. The nurses called him up and he just cut loose screaming and shouting. He stretched out like a flat board. Then they called me, "Grady Powell," and I went up. I put my arm out. It was the first time I ever had a needle in my arm and yes, it did hurt, but I didn't cry, nor did I scream or shout like Junior Taylor. It really wasn't as bad as I'd thought it would be. Through it all, Mable was by my side, as she continued to be for many years to come. We walked back home from Westwood Ford. I had gotten my shots for school. What a relief!

In September of 1939, I was seven years old. I couldn't read. Toot could read; Irene could read; but I couldn't read. There were certain things that we had learned to recite. One was the Lord's Prayer. Mama or Daddy would say the Lord's Prayer and we would repeat after them. The children were not expected to say the prayer alone until they reached a certain age, or a certain maturity. Then you would recite it to prove you knew it. All the older children knew the prayer and could say it. Toot knew it and Mert knew it. Percy, Buster, and Mable were teenagers, so of course they knew the prayer. My parents trusted their knowledge of the prayer, but they had to see them get down on their knees. As the youngest children, Irene and I did not know it yet. There came a time, however, when we decided we knew it. Irene decided she was ready to try it. She got down on her knees and started: "Once upon a time there was a little man and a little woman and a little boy, who lived in a little house and his name was Johnny Cake." Mama said, "No, Irene, you don't know it!" Irene thought the Johnny Cake story was the Lord's Prayer, and she was being as sincere as she could be. We teased Irene for the rest of her life!

As time went on, we learned to say the Lord's Prayer. As I look back on my life, the reciting of the Lord's Prayer with my family was the beginning of my lifelong journey with the Bible, and even to this day, when I say my prayers, I get down on my knees just like we did down in Brunswick County at my little home.

I remember, as a child, sleeping with Mom and Dad. The other children were sleeping upstairs. Mom and Dad decided that I was getting too big to sleep with them, but there was no other bed for me. So Mama decided to build me a bed. She went out and got some wood and got her handsaw, some nails, and a hammer. She also went out and got some guano sacks. Guano sacks were bags that fertilizer came in, and we didn't throw them away but would instead wash them and make underwear and other items, like skirts for Irene and Mable. While Mama was making the bed, the joke was on me because I said, "Mama, can I get in your pigpen?" (because I had never seen anything like it except a pigpen). Mama cried and said, "Lord, I don't even have a bed for my baby!" So Mama made me a bed with a mattress made of guano sacks. The bed must have been about twelve inches high, and I would enjoy that bed so much! I would climb up and get on that mattress and I had a little quilt. I finally had my own separate bed and I stayed in that bed until I started elementary school.

After I started elementary school at Westwood Ford, my sleeping arrangement changed. I went upstairs and I had to sleep with Mable and Irene. So there were three of us in one bed and I slept at the foot. My head was toward the foot of the bed, and Irene's and Mable's heads were toward the head of the bed. I slept there with them until three persons left home: Buster went to the navy; Mable went to Newport News; and Percy went to the sawmill, where they had shanties to sleep in. Finally, Irene had a bed to herself and so did I. I took the bed Buster had slept in. It was the bed Daddy had brought home from World War I.

My earliest work experience was on the farm. I must not have been more than eight or nine years old when Daddy took me out on the farm to drop fertilizer, which had to be done before the planting. He would come behind me with the mule and plow and turn that fertilizer into the ground. My mother protested. She said her baby was too young for that. "Come on, Grady, come on," my Dad would say. Then they got me a big straw hat. I didn't feel oppressed. I felt kind of proud that I was becoming a big boy.

As I said, my closest friend other than my siblings was my first cousin, Wilbert Pair (his mother, Aunt Pink, was my father's sister). We called him Samp. I didn't learn until the 1990s why we called him Samp. I was pastor of a church in Petersburg at the time, and his sister called me and wanted me to come down to Ante to have dinner because Samp was visiting from California, where he now lived. She had prepared the biggest dinner and Samp and I just laughed together for I don't know how long. We talked about girls we had dated and about playing together as youngsters. We talked about the choir in which we'd sung. We talked about Rev. Harrell, our beloved pastor. We talked about everything. Samp's sister said she looked out the door and saw us having the best time: our arms were flinging and we were just laughing. I said to him, "How did we come to call you 'Samp'?" He said, "You never heard, Grady?" He said it was one of the saddest stories of his life, because his mother used to fuss at him, and she would always finish by saying, "When you were born, you were so big that it almost tore me up!" So she called him "Sampson." Samp said he felt so bad that he "tore his mother up," and she made him feel worse about it.

Samp and I were together every day until we finished high school. We finished high school at sixteen years old, because we had seven grades. It was 1946. It was then that we went our separate ways. Samp went to the army and I went to college.

CHAPTER TWO

The Schoolteacher and Poplar Mount Members

There were many people who influenced me in Brunswick County. One of the towering figures of influence at that time was Lassie Austin. She was my teacher for seven years. As I look back, I see she did some great things.

There were no teachers in my immediate family. My first cousin Warner Pair married Mary Jones, who had been a teacher at James Alvin Green School. I didn't know there was such a thing as Standard English until I met Mrs. Jones.

I was simply in awe of teachers. I remember one day Mrs. Austin took off her shoes. She had to walk to school and had obviously stepped in some mud or something. I looked curiously at her feet because I didn't know if teachers' feet were the same as my mother's feet, but her feet looked just like Mama's! Now that sounds silly, doesn't it?

Mrs. Austin was wonderful. I remember that we had a small corner of our classroom that was used as our library, and Mrs. Austin encouraged us to read often. One book I remember was *Mother Goose Rhymes*. In it was "Little Jack Horner." It seems like just yesterday that I was sitting down reading in that little library area. I remember it so vividly . . .

Little Jack Horner sat in his corner, eating his Christmas Pie
He put in his thumb and pulled out a plum
And said what a good boy am I!

Mrs. Austin was our only teacher and taught six subjects: history, English, arithmetic, reading, writing, and geography. The thing I remember most about Mrs. Austin was something that changed my life. She said we were going to have a "word-a-day" book. It was really a word for the week, but she called it a word-a-day. She said she wanted us to use that word throughout the week so we could learn new words. All of us had to do it, all the grades, and we had to write it down in our books. The first word she gave us was "assume," and she said it meant "to take for granted." She explained that it isn't something you know. "If you see a snake," she said, "you would *assume* the snake is poisonous and it will harm you." She said, "All snakes are not poisonous. We don't have many snakes around here that are poisonous. If you assume that all snakes are poisonous, you take it for granted that they are and are not going to take any chances with any snake you see." She continued to elaborate on snakes and our "assumptions" about them, and when she had finished, we all knew the meaning of the word "assume."

We would often finish our lunch quickly so that our teacher would allow us to go outside and play. We did not have physical education classes, so baseball was our chance to play and have some recreation. We would choose players. I would always choose Blanch Claiborne. Blanch Claiborne, a girl, could hit a ball just like a boy. "I choose Blanch," was always the first thing you would hear. Leroy and I were usually selected as captains: I would choose this person and he would choose that person. One day they beat us but we didn't have our last inning. If I had the first inning, then Leroy would have the last and vice versa. On the same day, Leroy had the first inning and my team was supposed to have the last inning, but Mrs. Austin rang that bell. *Ding-a-ling-a ling.* We had to go in, and Leroy's team was just taunting us. "We beat you, we beat you!" they hollered. I replied, "I *assume* that no one won because we didn't have our last inning!" After we entered the school, everyone got quiet. Mrs. Austin said, "Grady, come up to my desk." Why? I wondered. Why was she calling me? So, I went up to the desk. It was not as if I had a choice. I was nervous. She said, "I heard you use a word coming in. What was that word?" I thought she meant I used a bad word. She said, "Didn't you use a word?" I said, "Nome." That meant "No ma'am." I was afraid. She said, "Yes you did, Grady. You used our word for the week! What's that word?" I said, "Assume." She said, "Now listen, class. Here is Grady in one of the lower classes, and I haven't heard anyone in the seventh, sixth, or fifth grades use that word, and Grady is using the word." I felt like a king! My fear had turned to joy! My chest just went out. She said, "Now class, I want you to do what Grady has done!" I walked back to my desk as if I were walking on air!

As Irene and I walked home that afternoon, we made a pact and decided we would correct each other when we did not speak correctly. We said we would stop splitting verbs. That's what we called it when you speak incorrectly. It wasn't splitting verbs; it meant anything that wasn't correct. So as Irene and I started on our way home, I would jump on her anytime she "split verbs." When we went out in the field to chop weeds, I would correct her, and in everything we did together, I would correct her. I was very aggressive in our little Standard English game and I guess I wore her out with it. She finally said she didn't want me to correct her anymore. I got on her nerves with it, but that began my lifelong quest to speak correctly and to pronounce words properly. When Bertie and I raised our children and they were very young, we would always correct them if they didn't use Standard English or didn't pronounce words correctly. I guess that tradition never really stopped with our children, even unto this day. Just the other day, I corrected my son Grady, Jr., who is now a grown man, when we were on the phone together and he mispronounced the word "pamphlet." As he continued to speak, I dashed to get my dictionary and explained to him that he was leaving out the "ph" in his pronunciation. He just laughed intensely as he pronounced the word properly over and over again to my satisfaction, because he knows this is something his dad enjoys. I was correcting him just as I corrected Irene in our little game many, many years ago! I just love the power of words when they are used correctly and spoken correctly. To this day, I do the Jumble in the newspaper every day.

In Brunswick County, when I was a youngster, we did not use Standard English outside of school. We would use expressions like "you was," "he ain't," or "she had did," and pronounced some words differently—for instance, "there" became "dair." In school, Mrs. Austin would correct us, but our parents did not use Standard English; our siblings didn't use it; Aunt Pink didn't use it. The one person in the family who did use Standard English was Mrs. Mary Jones Pair, and she always talked differently.

My father noticed that I was talking differently and I guess it was getting on his nerves, too. One day he was talking to me about chores on the farm. One of my chores was to "stob" the cow, which meant taking the cow out and putting a stake in the ground. You would tie the cow's chain to the stake so the cow could eat all around it. We were supposed to secure the cow so she wouldn't go into the wheat fields or anywhere else but where we wanted her to go. As I went about the job of "stobbing" the cow, my dad shouted out to me, "Grady, where is the cow?" I replied, "She's out there." He responded by saying, "Well go out THERE and get her!" He was mocking the way I pronounced "there," and it hurt my feelings badly. Time, however, would change this, because when I became a respected preacher, my Dad was so proud of me and the way I spoke. For many years as a pastor, I always encouraged youngsters to get an education. All this began with a teacher in Brunswick County by the name of Lassie Reavis Austin, to whom I am forever grateful.

Another interesting thing about Mrs. Austin was that she was in college while I was in high school, and she didn't graduate until 1946. I was going to high school when I saw my elementary school teacher on the campus of Saint Paul's, which at that time was a high school and a college. I believe seeing Mrs. Austin on campus gave me the idea that I could also go to college. So after high school, I became the first and only child of Herbert and Lillie to enter college.

There was one other educator who strongly influenced me in elementary school. Surprisingly enough, it was Mrs. Austin's father, Mr. Haywood Reavis. Mrs. Austin got sick once and went to John Hopkins Hospital in Baltimore, Maryland. It was the first time I'd heard of this hospital. We were told she had to have surgery. So her father came and took over her class for what must have been about four to five months. Mr. Reavis was with the first graduating class from Virginia Norman Industrial Institute, which today is known as Virginia State University. He had retired in 1939.

I remember Mr. Reavis very vividly. He used to say, "If you don't do that, I'll give you a whipping! Yes I will! Yes I will!" He never, however, spanked anyone. There was another fantasy he told us that I believed back then, but now I know was not true. He told us that you could command a table to move and it would move. So he had a table that must not have been more than three feet. He said, "Everybody come and put your hands on the table. Now put your thumb under the table with your finger on top of it." He said he then could command the table to move. Then he would proclaim, "Move, table!" He shook the table and it started moving back and forth. We thought the table was moving at his command. What a laugh he must have had when he would go home in the evening and think of us children and the moving table trick!

The other thing I remember about Mr. Reavis was that every morning at the beginning of the school day, he would recite a quotation that we had to learn from him. He would say things like, "A man without an idea is like a ship without a rudder." Another one that has stuck in my memory was "Old wretched man that I am, who shall deliver me from the body of this death?" by Dr. C. B. W. Gordon. I learned later that Dr. C. B. W. Gordon was from Petersburg. He was the pastor of Tabernacle Baptist Church, which is still active today. Dr. Gordon was asked to come to Brunswick County back then and preach once a month, every third Sunday, and that was his famous sermon. "Old wretched man that I am, who shall deliver me from the body of this death?"—that's from the Bible. We learned that quotation as schoolchildren. Each one of us would also have to stand and recite a Bible verse or other saying under the tutelage of Mr. Reavis. I would always say, "God is love."

Back then, no one cared about the separation of church and state. As long as black folk didn't bother white folk, they didn't care what we did. In fact, every Friday, we had a Sunday school lesson right there in the classroom! As the years went by and Bertie and I would sit down at the Sunday table with our young children at 312 S. Dunlop St., each one of them would recite a Bible verse before we ate. Grady Jr., who was about six or seven years old at the time, would always say, "God is love." I had passed on that tradition to my children.

Old Mr. Reavis carried on that class for his daughter while she was sick and he had a strong influence on me. May blessings be on his soul.

My earliest impressions from being in church came from Poplar Mount Baptist Church, where my father was a deacon and my mother was one of the "lead singers." I was impressed by several people at Poplar Mount. One was Charlie Vaughn. He spoke differently, not always correctly, but it impressed me. Charlie Vaughn was the grandson of a slave master and the slave master gave him an opportunity. Charlie Vaughn's father, the slave master's son, had a lot of land, on which he had a store. It was the only store I knew of that was owned by a black person. It was located in Fitzhugh, Virginia, which was no more than four miles from us. Charlie Vaughn was chairman of the deacon board of Poplar Mount Baptist Church. He would stand at church and say things like, "And we gonna . . ." He didn't say, "We are going to . . ." But he said it in a kind of nice way. I was impressed with him as a leader.

I was impressed by a lady named Bell Kelly. If there was ever a spiritual mentor in my life, it was Bell Kelly. First of all, she was always so clean, even though she was the wife of a farmer. Sometimes they would have a dinner to which others would be invited, and Mrs. Kelly would invite some young people as well. She would always have such a clean handkerchief! Her handkerchief was made of guano sacks, but when she would take it out, it was always so clean, you know?

Even though we had a preacher at Poplar Mount only once a month, we would still gather together every Sunday and carry on the business of the church; and oh how we would sing! Mrs. Kelly would do what we called "witness the preacher." Every third Sunday she would stand and say things like, "The Lord be praised!" She would talk about hymns and she would get up and say, "We don't have no hymns like old Dr. Watts!" I didn't know who Dr. Watts was, but apparently Mrs. Kelly did. We sang hymns. Irene and I would go home and sing them afterward: "What a Fellowship," "I Am Thine, Oh Lord," "Amazing Grace," "Remember Me."

We sang those songs in church and we sang other songs you didn't find in books. Mrs. Kelly's sister was named Virginia. We called her Miss Jenny and she was a wonderful singer! When she would sing, people would just pat their feet on the floor:

He's a wonderful Savior,
He's a lamp light under my feet; Oh a wonderful Savior,
he makes my joy complete.
He makes my pathway grow brighter, and my burdens
grow lighter,
What a wonderful Savior is he!

Mrs. Kelly would always sing "Remember Me." That was her song. My mother would sing "This Little Light of Mine." Oh how I remember Bell Kelly, Miss Jenny Gillus, Miss Mattie, and Elizabeth H. Green! What wonderful people they were!

I became very interested in Bible reading because of Mary Jones Pair. I mentioned her earlier because she married my cousin Warner Pair. She was a teacher who had tremendous influence on me and strongly urged me on in Bible reading at a very young age. I am so thankful for the multiple levels of influence she had on me! She lived on the same road as we did. Not only on Sunday, but every day, she spoke Standard English.

Another early influence was Helen Alexander Greene, because she taught in Sunday school. She was also a schoolteacher. She was the sister of William Alexander. I remember being impressed with her. We called her Miss Alexander. When we kids were told that Albert Greene was courting her, we thought it was a big deal that a schoolteacher would be courting anyone! I remember one Sunday he brought her to Poplar Mount, and I watched them because I didn't know how anyone would court a teacher. They would just talk and laugh! Although Helen was a member of the African Methodist Episcopal Church, like her brother, she joined our church and she and Albert were married. When a person from another denomination joined Poplar Mount, he or she had to be baptized by immersion.

Therefore, Helen Alexander Greene was baptized at Poplar Mount with me and sixty-three others.

As my Sunday school teacher, she impressed me greatly because she would say things so clearly! Her enunciation was so accurate. She would say things like, "And that's it! Yes!" I remember her teaching Sunday school, just like it was yesterday. She was so kind. She shared her knowledge and she made the Holy Bible come alive by her illustrations and examples.

Another influence in the "late morning" period of my life was Mrs. Mattie Claiborne. We called her Miss Mattie, and she was a very religious woman. She believed in a daily walk with God, the sanctity of marriage, and a variety of other Christian principles. I remember her telling one young man, "You shouldn't leave home and not tell your wife where you're going! It's ugly and it's not right!" She believed in honesty and truth. Her testimonies at Poplar Mount Church, through tears, were grounded in her belief in a daily walk with God.

There were many people who influenced and encouraged me at Poplar Mount. I started to become very interested in the activities of the church, and my father would take me with him to various church meetings since he was a deacon. There were those who could see that I was moving in the direction of becoming a preacher, and they encouraged and gave me church work to do. Rev. Harrell, for example, was our pastor, but he lived in Newport News, which was miles away from our church. He didn't come to Poplar Mount but once a month. He would come up on the third Saturday and stay with someone Saturday night and preach on Sunday. He would always say, "Y'all gonna hear from Grady! Ya hear! One day, y'all gonna hear from Grady!" That made me feel special and important. I wasn't more than fourteen or fifteen years old and encouragement like that means a lot to a child of that age.

When I was in Sunday school, they would call on me to make a statement. They would send me to the Bethesda Union, where I would speak on a given subject. The Bethesda Union was a Sunday school union. It was made up of about fifteen to twenty churches. It met every fifth Sunday at one of the member church schools. The program had an early afternoon youth division program. Every member church had to send a youth to participate. So, often, I represented Poplar Mount.

I was talking recently to Bessie Johnson Smith about those old times. She said, "Grady, you remember these things because your daddy bought you to church every Sunday. My daddy didn't go to church." She's right about my father's influence on me. I was going with my father to church meetings, worship, and other events, and I was gaining interest in the life and work of the church. At the age of fourteen, I knew that I was going to become a preacher.

One day, Poplar Mount announced that the Bethany Association meeting was coming up. The Bethany Association was an annual gathering of about forty churches. It was a grown folks association. By this time Rev. Harrell was no longer pastor at Poplar Mount; thus we had no pastor. Brother Vaughn said, "Whom shall we send to be our delegates to the Bethany Association?" Someone said, "I nominate Deacon Robinson." Someone else got up and said, "I nominate Brotha' Grady Powell." At the age of fifteen, I was selected to go to the Bethany Association, a grown folks meeting! It was September of 1947. What a time to remember, because, in a sense, I had arrived! I would be representing the whole church, not just the youth.

Around the time that I was selected to go to the Bethany Association meeting, Uncle Warner died. He was my father's brother. My father had stayed with Uncle Warner as a youngster because my dad's father died when he was only eight years old. Uncle Warner was crippled on one side. He could walk a little bit but would have to put his hand into his pocket to pull his leg around. As Uncle Warner got older, he couldn't walk, and he would always come down to Daddy's house on the wagon. After Uncle Milas's death, Uncle Warner had raised Milas's children: Johnny Powell, Adolphus Powell, Mae Powell, and Milas Powell, Jr. It's interesting that out of this line came Cleo Powell, Milas Powell's granddaughter, who serves as a judge on the Virginia Supreme Court, the first black woman to serve on that court. She was appointed in July of 2011.

After the funeral, I had to get to the Bethany Association meeting. My mom asked Mr. Bond, the funeral director, if he would take me to Emporia after the funeral and he said yes. Back then, people didn't eat or congregate after a burial, so I got into the car with Mr. Bond after Uncle Warner's funeral and was on my way to the Bethany Association! He took me to Emporia, where I was to catch a bus to Stony Creek. I was very excited because it was like I was going to Hawaii or New York. Everyone was proud of me and I beamed with anticipation.

I knew I was to get on the bus and go to Stony Creek. The bus seemed so big. I had never been on a commercial bus, and, for that matter, I had never been out of Ante, except on Christmas Eve when my sister Irene and I would go with Mable to Emporia, or when I went to the doctor's office in Emporia when Irene was sick. It took about forty-five minutes to get to Stony Creek. I was riding Trailways on a two-lane highway, Highway 301. The first thing the driver said was "Jarratt! Jarratt!" I knew that wasn't my stop. I noticed people would ring the bell when they wanted to stop: *Bling!* Then, the driver would stop at the next stop so they could exit. He left Jarratt and got back on 301, and it wasn't ten minutes before he said, "Stony Creek! Stony Creek!" I got right up with my little bag and I walked to the front. I was going to what I thought was the big city of Stony Creek. I walked out the door and it was pitch-black dark and I had no idea where I was! Lost at night in the middle of nowhere at fifteen years old. It wasn't a big city at all but a little country stop. "What am I going to do?" I thought to myself. "The meeting is supposed to be at a church, but there's no church in sight and it's pitch black outside!"

I walked to a general store, went in, and saw just a few people inside. I asked the person standing at the counter, who was white, "Sir, have you ever heard of Hunting Quarter Baptist Church?" He did not answer. A black man who was standing close by, however, spoke right up. "I have!" he replied. "We on our way to da 'sociation. You wanna go?" he asked. I said "Yeah!" So he took me in his car with his family to Hunting Quarter Baptist Church. It was about five or six miles outside of Stony Creek proper. At the time, people who went to these association meetings didn't have motels or hotels in which to stay. The association would have a committee to make arrangements for all of the delegates to stay overnight. When the meeting at Hunting Quarter closed that evening, Rev. Shands, the moderator, began to match up local church members with visitors: "Now all of you who need housing just sit right here because we gonna send you to where you will stay this evening."

When I arrived at my hosts' home, I was very happy because there was a young lady there. There I was all the way on the other side of the globe, as it were, in Stony Creek, and I got to meet a girl from Stony Creek. That made me important. We were at the house by 8 p.m. The association didn't have activities at night. Well, some young man came down from Petersburg or someplace and took her away! I guess he took her to Petersburg. I don't know where he took her, but I certainly was disappointed. That left me there with the old folks! Deacon Robinson and the people of the house just talked and I kind of joined in, and that's where I stayed for two days.

Mama had made me a pair of pajamas from some cloth she'd gotten somewhere. I guess she got it from the Ante Store, because they sold everything. The pajamas had sleeves on them, and she told me I was to wear them at night. This was the first time I had ever worn pajamas, and they were so short, my stomach was exposed. Since I had never worn pajamas, they were fine. How good I felt, an associational delegate grown up, sleeping away from home, and enjoying the good food of my host. The only thing missing was the host's girl, who had been taken away!

That was my first-ever experience representing anything or anybody. After the convention, Deacon Robinson arranged a ride home for us. The next third Saturday, he and I were to deliver a report to Poplar Mount on the associational meeting, and we did. That was my first time standing and reporting to that large church body, just as any adult would. I'd begun down a road that would lead and continues to lead me to speaking in front of large groups. Upon reflection, I see that the divine light that propelled me then continues to beckon me today.

Prior to the Bethany Association meeting, I had stood before a congregation, but had done so on a child's level. There was an organization known as the Bethesda Sunday School Union, and our Sunday school was a part of it. Our Sunday school would select five or six young people and they would read a paper or a scripture, recite a poem, or sing a song. We would go back to our congregation, stand, and say that we had represented the church. But with the Bethany Association, I was reporting as an adult, not a child!

CHAPTER THREE

Call to the Ministry

It was during my four years at Saint Paul's High School that I first felt compelled to preach, a feeling that motivated me to mature. So I preached my trial sermon before I finished high school. I began to seriously question around that time whether God had called me to be a preacher. The old preachers around me made me so frightened. They said, "Now if God didn't call you and you try to go, you'll never amount to anything." I got the idea that God would call out of the sky, but I had never heard any voice. I had never seen any light. It was in my soul, however, that I had to preach, and it was so much in my soul that I was embarrassed. I had to preach but I didn't want to preach. I think the main reason I didn't want to preach was because I wanted to be like the other boys my age. What girls would like a preacher? I thought being a preacher was an "old dote" thing and I didn't want to preach, but it was on me. It was so much on me that Daddy knew it and Mama knew it, and at church the people would encourage me, saying, "This boy is going to be something!" Rev. Harrell would say, "You're going to hear from Grady one day," and that made me feel that preaching was what I was supposed to do.

Well, God finally "spoke" to me while I was out in the farm fields. This happened in my own simplistic way, but for me, at the time, it was all the convincing I needed.

My lifelong passion for gardening started at a very young age. My father would have all his children out on the farm very early in the morning, doing our day's work in the field. We grew everything we ate. We grew wheat for our bread. We had chickens on the farm for our chicken and eggs. We had cows for milk, butter, and beef, and we had pigs for pork.

Daddy was the only one, however, who would slaughter the animals when it came time to do so. We had apple trees and grew corn. We were self-sufficient.

I became convinced that I had to preach when I was out on the farm doing my duties. Every morning before I went to school, I had a job. I had to milk the cow, take her out into the field, put a stave in the ground, and tie the chain to that stave so that the cow could eat circularly. Sometime during the day, my father would change it. I was the one, however, who had to start the cow off. Every day I would have to go get the cow and bring it back to the stable or the cow pen, as we would call it, and take up the stave and put it where I thought I would find it the next morning. Because the bus picked us up at 7:15 A.M., I didn't have much time. I had to milk the cow, eat, take the cow out in the field, and be ready to board the bus.

One morning I went out and I couldn't find that stave. I looked and I looked. I challenged the Lord in my simple way. I was still around fifteen years old and I said out loud, "Lord, if you have called me to preach, let me find that stave!" I walked right up on it! It sounds silly now, but for me, back then, it was a divine omen. Since then, I have never questioned my call to preach. Sounds incredible, doesn't it? Yet, that experience and others cause me to believe that God meets us where we are.

It was then that the challenge came. I was a junior in high school and our advisors wanted to prepare us to become seniors. One of our tasks was to write what we wanted to be. I didn't want to write "preacher," because I was reluctant to let my friends, especially the girls, know. My best friend Samp was very popular. He liked the girls and the girls liked him. I liked the girls, too, but I was to be a preacher, and I didn't want the girls to know I wanted be a preacher. So when the time came to write what we wanted to be, I wrote, "Christian education worker." I was always very interested in words and I thought that sounded sophisticated. This information was to go in a yearbook.

My advisor's name was Rachel Powell Stith, no relation to me. She was from Macedonia Baptist Church and taught English. She said to me, "Grady, after class I want to see you." "Yes ma'am," I said. I wondered why she wanted to see me. It worried me a little. Teachers were in a position of great authority over us. So after class, she said, "Pull up a chair and sit down. Grady, I have been reviewing these slips you students wrote and on yours you wrote 'Christian education worker.'" Lord, I didn't want to hear that, because I could see where she was going. I was hoping I could give a quick response and dash out of the room. She said, "Grady, do you want to be a preacher?" I said, "Yes ma'am." She said, "Sit down. I want to tell you something." She went on to talk with me about what being a preacher meant and how important it was to her. I didn't know she was a Christian. I had never seen her at church. She said, "Let me tell you, I want you to stay in school. One day you're going to come back and you're going to be standing at the pulpit and I'm going to be in the audience and you're going to be teaching me! Grady, it's the most honorable profession in the world, and don't be ashamed to tell people you want to preach."

"Great day in the morning!" I said to myself. That's what I needed to hear, and when I left Mrs. Stith's room, I was as happy and free as any man could be. The meeting was in a place called Webster Hall. If I could have walked a ladder four flights up and got on the top of the building, I would have waved my hands and shouted, "Listen all my fellow students and teachers, I want to be a preacher!" That's how good I felt, and from that day on, I have felt a degree of satisfaction about being a preacher.

After that experience, I was ready to announce my intentions to Poplar Mount and give my trial sermon. I told my daddy this and he said, "You got to go to the church meeting and tell it." So, I went to the church on Saturday, before the business meeting, and my dad and I talked to Deacon Charlie Vaughn, the chairman of the deacon board. Deacon Vaughn was ready to make the announcement. This was my moment: my trial sermon would be given after the announcement and acceptance from the participants. On that day, my life took a new direction. It was April 1950 and I was seventeen years old.

At the conclusion of the church meeting, Deacon Vaughn said, "We have brother Grady Powell here and he has said the Lord has called him. I'm recommending today that the church would hear him to see what we think about it. What shall we do?" Somebody made a motion that I should have the privilege to do my trial sermon. The motion was seconded and Brother Vaughn said, "Come on up for your trial sermon."

Well, I'd known that I would be asked to give my trial sermon and I was prepared for it. Daddy had told me to be ready. I had my little book and my little notes. There were about twenty-five to thirty people present.

The day is still so clear in my mind. After Deacon Charlie Vaughn told me to come forward for my trial sermon, I made my way up to the rostrum for what would be the first of many times to come. I was so nervous, I tell you the truth. I was glad they didn't have windows behind the rostrum at Poplar Mount because I think I would have jumped straight out the window!

I preached on the biblical subject of "Know ye not that your body is a temple of the Holy Spirit and you are not your own." This scripture can be found in 1 Corinthians 6:19. I used that as a subject and tried to convince them that I was not my own, that I belonged to God. I said that I think God has priority over me and over what I want.

When I finished my sermon, somebody stood up and moved that I should get my license to preach. I think it was Ms. Kelly. She said, "I move that Brother Powell should be given his license from this church!" It was seconded and carried. The church just went into tears. I still get emotional when I think about that day. Ms. Mattie Clayburn came up to me with tears rolling down her face and said, "Grady, I believe in you and you do right," and she gave me fifty cents. I don't know why in the world I didn't keep that fifty cents. I should have framed it, but I needed it so bad I spent it. It was Poplar Mount Baptist Church that gave me not only my license to preach but also the buoyancy that made me feel that I was *somebody*. Suddenly, at seventeen, I was a preacher.

High school was a most pleasant experience. All of my teachers inspired our minds, lifted our sights, and planted seeds that have borne fruit in myriad ways. The teachers were great. A dozen pages would be added to this book if I gave those who meant so much to me the commendations they deserve. Among those would be E. D. Adkins, H. Arnold Taylor,

O. G. Walker, Catherine James, Rachel Powell Stith, and so many others. E. D. Adkins was a major influence on me and I will discuss some of his influence later in this book. Also of special note was Mrs. Catherine James, the music teacher. She opened my eyes to the library of music and music education. Her classes were exciting; her choral teaching was superior and really taught us about music.

What a joy also to remember some fellow students. On our bus were Dorothy, Samp, and Evelyn (my cousins), my sister Irene, my brothers Mert and Toot, and others. Socially, times were happy. There was my girlfriend Dorothy Franklin, Jocelyn Maclin (my pal who later would become a cherished member of the church where I served as pastor), Stephen Brown ("Mr. Music"), Thomas Jefferson ("Einstein"), Bessie Johnson of Poplar Mount, John Burnett (now my neighbor), Lewis Evans ("Ping Pong"), and so many others who meant the world to me. What a pleasure! What a joy!

Brunswick County had not had a licensed black Baptist preacher in thirty years, so I became very popular and in heavy demand. I was preaching every Sunday. My daddy was so proud. I'd hear him say to people who wanted me to preach, "I don't know if you can get him . . . he's mighty busy!" I had to have a black book to keep up with my schedule.

In 1950, as I was getting ready to graduate from high school, I approached my father and said, "Daddy, I want to go to college." No one in my family had ever gone to college, and I was the youngest child. He was already impressed with me because I had begun preaching. He said, "Well, son, let me tell you. If you want to go to college, I'll work my fingers to the bone to see that you go." Those were his exact words. I'll never forget that moment.

Part II

Late Morning

CHAPTER FOUR

College Life and Meeting My Wife

So I finished high school and didn't have a suit. I asked Daddy about going to stay at Aunt Martha's house in Richmond so I could buy me some clothes for college. He thought that would be fine. I went to Aunt Martha's in the summer of 1950. She lived at 1821 W. Moore St., which was in an area of Richmond called "New Town." I bought what was my first suit. I bought a black suit, a corduroy coat, a pair of brown trousers, two sports shirts and a white shirt. Mable, my sister, bought me a pair of shoes, and that's what I went to college with.

In August, Daddy said, "We've got to sell some tobacco now." We never sold tobacco this time of year, but he wanted it sold early so he could have the money to send me to school. With a father looking out for his son and with the early selling of tobacco in August of 1950, I was able to enroll in college.

So I left Brunswick County and went on to college. I was the youngest preacher on the campus of Virginia Theological Seminary and College in Lynchburg, Virginia. I arrived the day after Labor Day. Eugene Woodruff took me by cab. My mother and father came, too. Liz Pair, my cousin, came just for the ride. For the first time, I saw the mountains of Virginia.

The second year I was there, my class elected me president of the lyceum. This school is now called the Virginia University of Lynchburg. I went to that school and met the president, Dr. M. C. Allen, who was also a dynamic preacher, and I met many other young and old preachers. There were about 200-250 preachers at Virginia Seminary, and here I was for the first time in my life thrown into a garden of preachers. Even now I sometimes think about them: Joseph Persons of Blackstone; Willis Henry and Russell Stonewall Jackson, both from New York; Elijah Hall of Washington, who happens to be my current neighbor; Isaac Williams; Charlie Moore; Charlie Hill (layperson); Mary Flenouy; Elma Patrick; and, during the last two years of Saint Paul's, Bill Holmes, Beatrice Garland, Wyman Colona, and Ellen Rice McGeachy.

Dr. Allen was the president of the Lynchburg school, and he would speak every Friday in the chapel. It was something to behold. He always spoke about the philosophy of that school, which centered on self-help and spiritual independence. He also made us feel that black was beautiful, which was very important to us all, coming from segregated backgrounds where whites would not even address black men as "Mr." He was a great influence on me. I remember distinctly his description of "Black." He stated that when a judge enters court, he wears a BLACK robe to show judicial authority. When the clergy wants to show divine authority, he or she wears a BLACK robe. The usual color of a pulpit Bible is BLACK. A mourning family member, he would say, wears BLACK. God dwells in the Negro Color; "No man has ever seen God." He dwells in the darkness. Only when blackness is in the color of one's skin do some people consider it as degrading. Dr. Allen would shout, "Black is honorable. Black is beautiful. Be proud to be black!"

Being in college was not only a big deal for me, but also for my family. As I said, no one in my family had ever been to college. My niece Ophelia has told me that when I was in college and would come home for a visit, everyone would get so excited because "Uncle Grady's coming home!" All my nieces, like Vivian, Lynnette, and Ophelia, my parents, and my brothers and sisters would gather around to visit and listen to me talk about college. Ophelia said it was as if God himself were there!

Time moved forward to the year 1952 and I met a young lady from Pittsburgh, Pennsylvania, who was also a student at Virginia Seminary and College. Her name was Bertie Mae Jeffress. Construction workers were repairing Graham Hall. This young lady sitting across the dining hall table from me really caught my eye. She was animated, personable. She was enjoying herself, chatting with others. She was very charming and I wanted to talk to her, so I said, "Would you pass me the salt, please?" I have jokingly told people that when she passed me the salt, I grabbed her hand and I haven't let go since! We walked out together talking and that's how I first met my wife, Bertie Jeffress from Pittsburgh, Pennsylvania.

When I met her, she let me know she had a boyfriend. But he was in Pittsburgh and she was with me in Lynchburg. At the time we met, Bertie was writing her name and his in her books: "Bertie Jeffress and William Henderson." Months later, her mother said, "When Bertie came home, I noticed she was writing in her book, 'Bertie Jeffress and Grady Powell.'" But her mother didn't know who Grady Powell was. Bertie told her that I was in Virginia and I was a preacher. I would later learn that her parents weren't too fond of Mr. Henderson anyway.

So Bertie and I started dating. When we were still courting, she left Virginia Seminary and College because her aunts, who were educators, convinced her mother that she needed to be at a four-year accredited college. They were shocked and dismayed that "Sug," her mother's nickname, had sent her daughter to an unaccredited four-year school, so she transferred to Virginia Union. Subsequently, I travelled to see her one Saturday. I hitched a ride with a fellow student who would be passing through Richmond on his way home that weekend. He took me to Aunt Martha's house. I wrote Aunt Martha and asked her if I could come, because Aunt Martha, I found out, lived very near Virginia Union. Bertie lived in a place called Porter Cottage at the time and she told me it was on Lombardy St. I walked from Aunt Martha's house to Lombardy. And there was a sign that said "Virginia Union University." At that point, I knew I was near the campus. I went to the first house on the left. Bertie had said it was to the left, but it was not Porter Cottage that I came to. It was at the home of Dr. John Ellison, the President of Virginia Union.

I rang the bell and the charming Mrs. Ellison answered the door. I introduced myself and she called her husband. "John, there's a young man here named Grady Powell. He has come to see Ms. Bertie Jeffress. He is from Virginia Seminary." Dr. Ellison literally ran down the stairs because he was very much against Dr. Allen. Dr. Allen had pretended that Virginia

Seminary was a four-year school. It was not. It was a two-year school, but he kept people there for four years and let them graduate. They couldn't get a teaching certificate, though. They were preachers. You see, he was training old men to preach, and when they finished Virginia Seminary, they didn't need to go any further. They had been educated, in the mind of Dr. Allen. Many preachers went to Virginia Seminary only because it was a seminary. When they finished four years of college, they could get a degree called the BTH, Bachelor of Theology. The Association of Theological Schools does not give that degree anymore. Years ago it gave the BTH when people weren't going to college.

Be that as it may, Dr. Ellison and Dr. Allen didn't get along because Virginia Seminary was not known as a great school of scholarship. It was known as a preaching school. Dr. Ellison's school was a school of scholarship. At certain conventions where both men would be present, many people would praise Dr. Allen and Dr. Ellison didn't like it. Dr. Allen was a dynamic preacher! Dr. Ellison told me that day in his home that Dr. Allen led the people wrongly. Dr. Allen stood one day at one of those meetings and said, "Some people are talking about the accreditation of schools. Let me tell you about accreditation of schools. God accredits schools!" All the people jumped to their feet, as Dr. Ellison listened in misery. Dr. Ellison said Dr. Allen knew that a denominational association cannot accredit schools—nor does God. The Southern Association of Schools and Colleges (SASC) does.

Anyhow, Dr. Ellison went on to tell me that day how I was wasting time going back to Virginia Seminary after two years. His question was, why didn't I go to Saint Paul's, which was accredited? He said I had already attended Saint Paul's High School. Why did I leave? I had never heard of accreditation. A college is a college is a college, as far as I knew. Under Dr. Ellison's influence, I left Virginia Seminary and returned to Saint Paul's College, where I had finished high school. That's the story of how I finished Saint Paul's College in 1954. I did, by the way, finally see Bertie that day at Porter Cottage, but only after that chance meeting with a man who would become my close advisor and friend: Dr. John Malcus Ellison.

In the summer of 1952, our relationship was becoming serious, so I went to Pittsburgh, Pennsylvania, to see Bertie and to meet her family. I traveled to Pittsburgh by train. Warner Pair took me to the Emporia train station. Mama had fixed me some chicken in a bag. I had on my suit. Oh, how I remember that trip. It was quite an experience. The train went around what was called Horseshoe Bend. It was winding around the mountains of Pennsylvania. When I got off the train, I saw Bertie standing there waiting for me. Standing by her was another young lady. Bertie said, "This is my sister Fay."

"How are you, Ms. Jeffress?" I said to Fay. I was real formal then.

I had unfortunately developed a very serious toothache on the train and when I told Bertie and Fay, Fay took me to the dentist. It was the first time in my life I had ever been to the dentist. We didn't go to dentists and doctors down in Brunswick County! Fay paid for this. Fay became a most important person in my life. She has been the kindest and most generous person I know.

Well, meeting Bertie's family, and most importantly her parents, went well. I asked her parents for permission to marry Bertie and they granted it. Therefore, in the summer of 1953, August the 29th, in Charlotte Court House, Virginia, at a little church called Beautiful Plains Baptist Church, Bertie and I were married. Bertie's mother, who was also named Bertie, was from Charlotte Courthouse, and Beautiful Plains Baptist Church was the church she'd attended in her youth. Bertie's father was also there. He was a member of Morrison Grove Baptist Church. Bertie selected Charlotte Court House rather than Pittsburgh so that my family could come to our wedding. My parents and family were in attendance. It was a day I'll always remember. There they were, Dad, Mom, sisters and brothers.

PART III
Noonday

Chapter Five

Preaching Beginnings

When I got to Saint Paul's College, I was already a preacher. I had become well known in the local area. I had been to Virginia Seminary and I had been preaching constantly. I had taken a class called Effective Preaching at Virginia Seminary, and T. H. E. Jones of Saint Paul's allowed me to substitute Effective Preaching for Public Speaking, a course they required. Several other courses were likewise substituted. This was important to me because I wanted to move on with my college career.

While I was at Saint Paul's College, I was called to my first church. Someone told me I had some mail. I went up to the post office and here was a post card written in pencil. It was from Mt. Zion Baptist Church in Green Bay, Virginia. I had never heard of the place. They addressed it to "Rev. Grady Powell, Saint Paul's College" and asked me if I would come and preach. They were looking for a pastor. I thought to myself, "Ah, oh my! I don't know where Green Bay is," and I went home and told Daddy.

I couldn't stay at home, so I stayed with Nurse Avent, a cousin of my daddy's, and would go home on Fridays. Mannie Pair and Joseph Claiborne would take me to wherever I was to preach.

One Sunday morning Mannie, Joe, Dad, Mom, and I made our way to Green Bay, Virginia. We went through Blackstone and on up to Burkeville. From Burkeville, we made our way into Green Bay. Mannie rolled down the window and asked a passerby, "Y'all know where Mt. Zion Baptist Church is?" "Yeah! Just go straight down that road. You can't miss it!" he replied. Finally we came upon Mt. Zion Baptist Church. The year was 1953 and I was nineteen years old.

I preached at Mt. Zion, and they liked me. They paid me nine dollars. Daddy said, "Umm, Grady, they don't take up much money do they?" Poplar Mount, my home church, was taking up about a hundred dollars in collections. Mount Zion collected eleven dollars, gave me nine, and kept two for themselves, but I was mighty grateful! They asked me if I would come back. Yes, I went back. The third time I returned, they asked me to be their pastor, and the Lord knows I wanted to be the pastor so badly, I didn't know what to do. We agreed. They agreed to pay me $12.50 twice a month, on the first and third Sundays. This payment would be comparable to a pastor's salary today.

In the meantime, however, while they were negotiating with me, another church in South Hill heard about me, and they also needed a pastor. The church's name was Amity Baptist Church. There was a lady by the name of Mrs. Simmons who was teaching in the elementary school department of Saint Paul's College. I was doing my student teaching at the time and I was with a teacher named Mrs. Street, whose class was next door to Mrs. Simmons's. Mrs. Simmons's husband was a member of Amity Baptist Church and he was the chairman of the deacon board. She told him about me, the young preacher at Saint Paul's College.

When I went to Amity to preach, they seemed very formal. They had little white robes like Episcopalians wear. One of the members, C. Edith Taylor, was a teacher, and she called me "Rev. Mr. Powell." Several members of the congregation were teachers with degrees. They called me as pastor two weeks after Mt. Zion called me. I wanted to be pastor of both churches, but Amity was the first Sunday and Green Bay was the first and third Sundays. I went to Mt. Zion in Green Bay and asked them if they would have their service at 1:00 P.M., because Amity had its service at 11:00 A.M. Mount Zion said they would do it. They didn't like it, but they did it for me.

In 1953, I purchased my first car. It was a 1949 Chevrolet and it cost $895. I was twenty years old. Since I had saved my money in a trunk upstairs, I was able to pay for my own car. For the down payment, Daddy signed for me to borrow the money from the bank in Emporia. I borrowed that and I had to pay something like eight to ten dollars per month. I don't quite remember exactly how much it was, but I borrowed $695 and paid the bank and paid for insurance. The way it ended up, I owed the bank in Lawrenceville forty dollars per month, and I made it because I spent my money wisely. I had to also pay the bank in Emporia. Yes, Daddy signed for me, but I had to pay every penny of the loan.

It's a wonder that I'm not dead, because I used to jump into my car in South Hill and I would hit those curves at sixty miles per hour on my way to Green Bay. I would go down through Forest, Virginia, all those country roads. It was about a twenty-five minute drive. Mama and Miss Sarah Clayburn would always go with me. Mama would say, "Grady, you're going right fast." Miss Sarah would say, "I just put my hands in the Lord! Haha! I don't care how fast he drives," and she would just laugh out loud as I dashed around those curves in my Chevrolet!

So now I had two churches. Mt. Zion paid me $12.50 a Sunday, which was twenty-five dollars per month. Amity paid me twenty-five dollars for one Sunday. My income was fifty dollars a month! I hadn't ever made any money like that in my life.

I had other engagements also. I was available the second and fourth Sundays, so I would preach at other churches. I was busy and loving it. I knew I would have fifty dollars from the two churches, so whatever I made from other engagements was beyond what I owed the bank. That caused me to save and to watch my money very closely. I have literally taken care of myself since I was nineteen years old.

Into the picture came a church called Macedonia. It was located in Greenville County, which was only about fifteen miles from my home. A man named Raymond Adams, whose daughter I had dated, was chairman of the deacon board at Macedonia and they had asked me to preach for youth Sunday. So I preached at Macedonia, and after the service Deacon Adams came and said, "Come here, young man."

He counted out money to me. "One, two, three, four, five, six, seven, eight . . ." and he continued, all in dollar bills. No one gave fives or tens. He continued counting and my heart starting beating faster! "Thirty-six, thirty-seven, thirty-eight, thirty-nine, forty. How's that?" Forty dollars for one Sunday! Forty dollars! That's the first time I had ever been paid that much for preaching. I folded it and put it in my pocket. That was a big day!

CHAPTER SIX

My Five Children

With so much reflection on my early years as pastor, it's hard not to think of my five children. Although each is referenced at various places, they are The Group—Our Jewels.

In November of 1953, Bertie became pregnant with Sandra. She dropped out of school because she became so sick. In spite of Bertie's sickness, the time was exciting. I would become a father. This was a new anticipation for my life. Excitedly, we talked about a name. At the time, the sex of a child was not known until the birth. If a boy, surely the name would be Grady W. Powell, Jr. If a girl, not another Bertie—there were already two—so we arrived at a name related to a person who had done so much for Bertie and had embraced me in such a wonderful way—her sister, Fay. We used Fay's middle name, "Zemoria," which also happened to be Aunt Irene's middle name. For the first name, we used "Sandra," a name that Bertie liked. Thus our firstborn is named Sandra Zemoria Powell.

Aunt Irene's husband was a medical doctor. Very willingly, he became Bertie's physician during her pregnancy. They lived in Chase City, Virginia. We moved to Ante, my parents' home, where we would stay until May 1954, my college graduation. After graduation we moved to Charlotte Court House, Virginia, into the home of my wife's late grandparents. There we were, the first time in a single home, just the two of us. It was a time of chopping wood, and serving as pastor of two rural churches, Mt. Zion and Amity. Just sixteen miles away were Aunt Irene and her husband, Dr. Pierce. The doctor's visit for Bertie's care was more than just medical. Aunt Irene, a strong educator and the principal of Historic Thyne Institute, loved us and taught me by example and direct instruction. Additionally, she was a great cook! Oh, the pork brains, the steamed cabbage, the rabbit and other wild game hunted by Dr. Pierce, and so much more.

Dr. Pierce had a close physician friend, Dr. J. J. Bates of South Boston, Virginia. Bertie would be turned over to him for delivery.

The morning of August 7, 1954 (one day after my twenty-second birthday), I took Bertie to South Boston Hospital, where Sandra arrived in the early afternoon. She was the prettiest baby I had ever seen! So now we had "Sandra Z", our eldest. She ignited a new chapter in our lives. We were now parents. The joys and challenges of growing up were kind to us by way of Sandra. Today she is Dr. Sandra Powell Mitchell, a strong educational administrator.

Her birth and subsequent life set the stage for the births of four more. Dorthula (Dot) Hamlette Powell was born in 1956 and was named after Bertie's aunt, who was Dorthula Hamlette. She was brought to Virginia Union University (VUU) two days old from Community Hospital in Richmond. This school, where she lived the first two years of her life, would later become her alma mater in 1978. Dr. Dorthula H. Powell-Woodson showers us with much appreciation. Today, she is partner in a law firm in Washington, D.C.

I left Emporia in 1956 to enroll in the School of Theology at VUU. We scheduled Bertie's return to VUU in 1957 so that we would graduate at the same time—she from college and I from the seminary. It worked!

When we both graduated, Bertie was expecting our third child. This time it was a boy! Here was Grady Jr., my namesake, who would carry the name and tradition of the Powells. He was born at Community Hospital in Richmond. He was robust, a typical boy growing up, athletically inclined and the first male, a most meaningful addition. His early growth years, high school and college, and his marriage brought me joy. He was popular, especially with the girls. Life changed. To the girls, I became "Grady's dad," not Rev. Grady Powell. Today, he is the author of two books, writes and plays music, and is employed at Comcast NBC Universal.

The fourth child was Herbert Conway Powell. Names are significant and his name falls in that category. His names come from his grandfathers:

Herbert was my father's first name and Conway was Bertie's father's first name. He blended these well. His strong leadership and good will have caused us to appreciate Herb's love and helpfulness to us, his parents, and likewise to his siblings. He's our pillar of strength; we say he's the boss of the family. At this moment, he has just completed the memoirs for Maurice White, the founder of the band Earth, Wind and Fire.

Our baby, Eric Charles Powell, was so named because of his health challenges from pre-birth. We chose the names Eric (gentleman) and Charles (strength) for their significant symbols. Those choices now seem prophetic. He is truly a gentleman whose strength has been shown as the years have come and gone. Time has come to prove that our faith in his development was correct. Today he is showing his strength as a counselor to persons in Los Angeles, California, who desperately need his knowledge, interpersonal relation skills, and his strength.

In 1977 my wife wrote a poem that expresses our joint thoughts about the children we have been blessed to bring into this world.

<u>My Children</u>

They are my jewels,
>Those dear and priceless gems,
>Which kings and queens revere,
>And guards do watching steer
The thieves from near their sight.
They are my joy,
>Those dear and priceless gems
>Which glow and glitter smiles,
>That prick the heart-string dials,
>To make me know their worth.
They are my life,
>Those dear and priceless gems,
>Which give me driving zeal,
>To make their highest wills
The goals for which I strive.

PART IV
Early Afternoon

Chapter Seven

Beginning Pastorates and Teaching Jobs

Time moved on without delay. This "early afternoon" portion of my life was filled with discovery and hard work. I had been called as pastor at Beautiful Plains Baptist Church and St. Louis Baptist Church. Both of these churches were in the Charlotte Court House community, within five miles of each other, so this worked well since Bertie and I were now living in Charlotte Court House. At that time I had pastorates that covered every Sunday of the month, as well as income from four churches. Amity had raised me to forty dollars a month. I was getting thirty dollars a month at Mt. Zion. At Beautiful Plains I was getting thirty-five dollars a month, and at St. Louis I was getting thirty dollars. Thus my total earnings per month were $135. This was great. It included an opportunity to serve the church and have money for my family.

Then in 1954, I finished at Saint Paul's College and started teaching. I signed a contract to teach in April of '54 before I finished in May. Ms. Stamps, the "colored" visiting teacher, signed me up. That agreement wasn't so smart, because I was later offered other, more appealing jobs. My fast decision to sign a contract was based on feeling so big because I had a contract in my pocket and none of my classmates did. However, I had a dilemma. I was going to teach, but it was for $1,900 annually, and I was offered a different teaching job that paid close to $3,000 annually in Orange, Virginia. There in Orange, I would be a teaching principal, and I wanted that job. So, I went to Emporia to ask the superintendant if I could be released from my contract. The Emporia superintendant told me, "Oh no! No indeed!" He explained that schools have a gentleman's agreement that applicants can't be fishing around for jobs, because they would mess school systems up if they start changing contracts at the last minute. So I had to go to Emporia to teach. I felt sad about this. I wanted more money. I needed more money. But let me tell you what my favorite hymn is:

All the way my Savior leads me. What have I to ask beside?
Can I doubt, his tender mercy, Who thru life has been my guide?
Heavenly peace, divinest comfort, Here by faith in him to dwell!
For I know, whatever befall me, Jesus doeth all things well!
　　Fanny J. Crosby

I didn't want to go to Emporia, but I had to go. It was the right thing to do. The money was low, but I was still preaching, and I believed in my heart that even though I fell into a quagmire, "Jesus doeth all things well." I knew God was on my side. I always felt God was watching over me.

Bertie, Sandra, and I lived in Charlotte Court House for only a brief period of time, about four or five months. I would travel back and forth from Charlotte Court House to Emporia, where I was now a teacher. At the beginning of each week, I would go to stay with my parents in Emporia while teaching, and Bertie and Sandra would remain in Charlotte Court House. Eventually, we all moved together to Emporia, but I would still have to drive back to Charlotte Court House to fulfill my obligations as pastor of Beautiful Plains Church and St. Louis Church.

I met a man named Rev. C. L. Evans, who told me I ought to go to seminary. He said I had so much promise. I met him in Kenbridge, Virginia. Meeting C. L. Evans was just a "chance meeting." I had preached at Beautiful Plains Baptist Church and was returning to Emporia. I suggested that we stop by to see Rev. and Mrs. Hayward Watkins, the pastor of St. Matthew's Baptist Church. I had come to know Rev. Watkins, a graduate of Virginia Union University and a fine pastor. We had become friends.

The Rev. C. L. Evans was the executive secretary of the Baptist Allied Bodies of Virginia, now the Baptist General Convention. One Sunday, Dr. Evans was guest preacher at St. Matthew Baptist Church. He talked with me about the seminary at Virginia Union University. He assured me

I could get in. They had scholarships for promising young men, and I could get an apartment on the campus. He gave me the name of Dr. Allix B. James, the dean. This was interesting to me because I wanted to be a full-time pastor, and not a teacher.

From his encouragement, I decided I was going to go to seminary. I gave up teaching in Emporia after two years and went for broke. I was still getting money from the churches, but I was driving too much. I had managed to save $600 while I was teaching and preaching. I took care of a wife, our baby Sandra and myself. I gave Mama money and paid my cousin Luther for living in his house.

I would have had $600 when I went to seminary, except the IRS got me and wiped me out. I did not know that preachers had to pay income taxes. Nobody ever told me. Most preachers out in the country were paid in cash. Nobody paid any attention to taxes. I just didn't know. When I got to seminary and took church administration, I learned about income taxes. Dr. Allix James was teaching and he invited some businessperson to come in and talk about income taxes. I could have gotten out of it, but I went down to the IRS on Main Street and told them that I had been a preacher and I had never paid any taxes. When the tax person finished he said, "Here's what you owe." It was about $300-$400 and I said, "Well sir, I don't have that." I told him I had very little money. He said, "Well, you have a car, don't you? We can take the car." I had to take the bulk of my savings account and pay the IRS, and I didn't ever have to tell them. People have said to me, "Grady, why did you tell them?" I would respond by simply saying, "I wanted to do right." Now that I see the tax structure and people making millions of dollars and not paying taxes, I think that would have helped my conscience. Had I known this, I am not now sure that I would have reported this.

I had made the decision, however, to go to seminary, as C. L. Evans had suggested, and I was going to go even though the IRS had pretty much wiped out my savings. So I moved to Richmond on a borrowed pickup truck belonging to Irving Reavis, who was a member of Poplar Mount. We had an oil stove, which I took to my parent's house to store, and we packed our bedding, clothes, and kitchenware. I put everything we owned on the truck, though we didn't have much. Then we were on to Richmond—my wife, my daughter, and me.

Bertie was expecting Dot. We already had Sandra, who was two years old, and we went for broke. I knew I had to go to seminary for three years. Bertie had two years more to finish college, so we made a plan. The plan was that while I did my first year of seminary, Bertie would take care of the children. After I completed my first year of seminary, Bertie would reenter college and we would both finish two years later, and we did it! The year was 1956.

Because of the timing of Dot's impending delivery, we could not go to Pittsburgh, Pennsylvania, that summer as we usually did. We therefore went to Lunenburg County for our vacation. I took one little girl and a pregnant wife. We returned to Virginia Union in August and on September 6, our second child was born. I registered for seminary on the next day. Dot was born at Community Hospital, and she slept her first night out of the hospital on the campus at Virginia Union University. It is ironic that some years later in 1974, she returned to Virginia Union and entered as a college student. She had returned to the place of her birth. She finished in 1978, lived in Richmond, and went on to T. C. Williams School of Law at the University of Richmond.

I continued preaching at four churches for the next two years and in 1958, Dr. James, Dr. Proctor, and Dr. Ellison told me that I shouldn't be serving four churches. They were my teachers and they convinced me that I should serve one church and use my talent to be the "pastor" of one church, not just preaching. I tried to do this. I wanted to live in Charlotte Court House and wanted Beautiful Plains Church and St. Louis Church to join together and become one church. They were just three or four miles apart. I went to Beautiful Plains first and talked to the deacons. The first thing I wanted them to do was endorse the idea of having worship twice per month—the second and fourth Sundays.

Have you ever talked to anyone who just looked at the floor while you spoke? That is what happened as I proposed my idea. I had hoped I could then go to St. Louis Baptist Church and ask them to have services on the first and third Sundays. My idea was if we did that for one year, I could get the churches to join together and become one congregation and call it Charlotte Court House Baptist Church. Did they take my suggestion? Absolutely not!

So I continued on for a while, preaching at four churches, but still holding on to Dr. James and Dr. Proctor's suggestion about finding one church and being a pastor instead of just preaching. I was talking with the deacons about having service twice per month, and by this time, they were paying me fifty dollars. Deacon Moses said, "Reverend, we pay you fifty dollars on the second Sunday. Would you want us to pay you fifty dollars on the fourth Sunday, too?"

We preachers have never liked talking about money, but we have to make a living. I responded to him by saying, "You really don't have to set a salary. I would be quite willing to come here and do everything I could do, and whatever offering was taken up, you would keep half of it for the church and give me half. If it was fifty dollars, then give me twenty-five." He said, "Rev. Powell, s'pose we took up $150. Then you'd be getting seventy-five."

When I heard him say that, something in me said, *Give it up. That's so stingy.* I thought it could have all worked out so well. I would have had a little village church. Also, I could have worked with Mother Zee, my wife's grandmother. She owned the Jeffress Funeral Home. I could have made some money working with them, and I would have had enough income. Bertie was finishing school and there was her grandparents' home where we could live. So I told Deacon Moses, "Let's think about that." I knew then that I was going to leave, and I started telling my story to Doctors James, Ellison, and Proctor.

The year was 1958. The "late morning" period of my life was slowly but surely approaching the "early afternoon." There was a lady teaching in Charlotte Court House named Sonata Lindsey. She was from Henrico County and was baptized at Quioccasin Baptist Church, where her daddy was a deacon. Sonata Lindsey knew about this young preacher out there where she was teaching and she told her dad. In addition, Rev. Ross, a native of Brunswick County living in Richmond, told Deacon Pryor, who was chairman of the deacon board at Quioccasin Baptist Church, about me. One evening the telephone rang. I had a telephone by this time! "Rev. Powell, this is Deacon Pryor, mmm, mm, Quioccasin. Rev. Ross told me 'bout you. Could you come and preach for us?"

"Yes sir!" I responded. I went out there to preach and I liked it and they liked me. It was fifteen minutes from Virginia Union University. It was four Sundays per month. I was a student and they called me to be their pastor. That was the first time I became a full-time pastor. I was able to resign from four churches: Amity in South Hill; Mt. Zion in Green Bay; Beautiful Plains in Charlotte Court House, and St. Louis Baptist Church in Phoenix, Virginia.

I was just twenty-four years old when I became pastor at Quioccasin. I was able to fulfill many desires through this church. For one thing, I wanted to become a part of one church family, as opposed to running from church to church just to give sermons. The church family at Quioccasin accepted me as a pastor. The older-aged persons accepted me, and the youth embraced me. I would drive over to be with them on Thursday nights for choir rehearsal and I would even sing with them a bit. Another desire that was fulfilled via Quioccasin was the fact that I was tired of driving all over Virginia to meet my obligations as preacher to four different churches. Driving sixty to seventy miles an hour trying to be on time at four different churches was wearing me out. With Quioccasin, I would just jump in the car and in fifteen minutes, I was at the church.

Quioccasin gave me an opportunity to begin experimentation with what it means to be a full-time pastor. I was called to Quioccasin in 1958, and I had a year and a half more to complete my seminary training. I could now begin to try some principles I was learning in seminary, particularly in church administration and worship. For example, I had already begun writing a church bulletin for Sunday worship when I was at the four rural churches. I had met a lady named Ms. Rawlings, who worked for Consolidated Bank & Trust, and she was a typist. I found her through John Cross, a classmate, who was her pastor. She typed a bulletin every Sunday for those four rural churches that I had resigned from. Because of that experiment, I wanted a secretary who would do the same thing at Quioccasin. I started out with Ms. Rawlings, but she could only do the bulletin if I wrote it out just as I would a class project. Very soon the church realized that I wanted a secretary. They hired a part-time secretary who was related to Deacon Overton, and she served me very well.

She would come in to the office in the early evening on Wednesday, so I would try to have an early dinner. I would dictate letters to her and get the bulletin prepared. I would come back on Saturday and she would run the bulletin on Saturday. I felt good about what I was doing and was getting the feel of being a full-time pastor. I would go to choir rehearsal and to deacons meetings. They had what was known as the "Deacons Club." It consisted of the deacons and their spouses. Every quarter they would have this big dinner. I enjoyed the eating, but more than the eating, I enjoyed just getting to know the people of the church I served. For the first time, I was really living with the people. The deacons gave me that opportunity through their meetings. Quioccasin had been a rural church; however, it was changing to a suburban church. I was the second pastor in this transformation. They were willing to experiment with new ministries and an expanded view of church life.

The ushers also organized themselves as a group. In the fall season, the ushers would take a trip to Skyline Drive to observe the changing of the seasons. They invited me to go. These are the kinds of things that gave me an opportunity to not only preach to people, but to get to know them. They were very kind for inviting me to their homes and helping me to know the young people. I organized the youth into a young people's society and I would go to church and meet with them. I had their phone numbers and would call them from time to time.

So my dream was coming true. I talked with them about my dream of being a full-time pastor and they talked with me about building a parsonage in order for me to be right there. We purchased a half acre of land right beside the church for $3,000, and they started building. It was going to be a trilevel home. I can't even convey how happy I was, and Bertie was happy, too! There are no words to describe what Quioccasin meant to me. They fulfilled my long-held desire to be a pastor. Although more than fifty years have passed, this church remains close to my heart today.

There was one problem. When I finished the seminary in 1959, Bertie also finished college. Quioccasin was not paying me enough money to support a family of four, and we were expecting our third child. So I began to seek a supplemental job. I didn't want to teach, so I didn't even apply for teaching jobs. I thought that being a social worker would be a good choice because I could do the necessary work of that job during the day, and at five o'clock, I could start the work of the church. Some people have been bivocational all their lives, so I knew I could do it for a little while without a problem. I could still go to the Deacons Club meetings and I could be at choir rehearsal. I could operate the youth society and work with my part-time secretary, who had always been at the church in the evening.

So I went to the social work department of Richmond, which was on Broad Street. I told them I wanted to apply and they invited me to do so, but said there were no vacancies. I went to apply as a social worker in Chesterfield and Henrico: no vacancies! I finally realized that I was being turned down because of the color of my skin. Well, I was devastated! My wife was pregnant with our third child and I wasn't making enough money. Here I had given up teaching in Emporia and gone to seminary for three years. I had finished academically at the top of my class. I had a full-time church but not enough money. The part-time job I was interested in as a social worker rejected me because I was black, and I was extremely sad about my situation. I was happy about Quioccasin and sad about money. That's a part of life, I know.

I was walking on 7th Street near Broad and was almost in tears. Something in me said, "Go by the school board office." I was desperate for a job and I went in. I went upstairs to the office of a man named Mr. Long. I told the secretary, who greeted me very nicely, that I was wondering if there were any vacancies in the city of Richmond for teaching jobs. She asked, "What is your field?" I said, "I just finished the seminary and I finished

Saint Paul's College in elementary education." She said, "I think you might be in luck, because we have been waiting for a man. Mr. Long has said that he wants a man in elementary education at a particular school that has all women. Have a seat and I'll tell him you're out here." I went into Mr. Long's office and he jumped up and said, "You're in elementary education?" I said, "Yes sir!" He said, "We need you! You finished Saint Paul's College?" I replied in the affirmative. He said, "Now, you'll have to understand that we are not hiring you for your seminary degree. That's wonderful, you made good grades, but we're not hiring you for that. We're hiring you because we need you as a teacher. There's a school in Richmond called Fairfield Court Elementary School where we need twenty-three teachers. We have twenty-two women and the principal is a woman, and I want to put a man in there." He continued by saying, "You see these. They are all applications, but they are all from women, and I need at least one man and I'd like to hire you. When can you start?" I said, "Tomorrow!" He replied, "All right! We'll start you tomorrow. Here's the contract. It's a one-year agreement."

The contract started me off with $2,600 a year: a ten-month school year, at $260 per month. I knew that was more than enough to take care of my family, along with the money from Quioccasin. I should have been the happiest person in the world. I now had enough money, but I left that office sad. My objective had been thwarted. I wanted to be a full-time pastor and here I was going back to teaching, which I gave up in 1956 in order to go to seminary for three years. I wanted to serve a church with my total dedication and it didn't happen. I was very hurt. I just wanted to preach and do ministry. Now teaching would take most of my time.

I went home and mustered up a kind of false joy to tell my wife that I had found a job. That afternoon, I drove to the school and met the principal, Mrs. Cooper. I was teaching sixth grade, and while I enjoyed the children, I was never, ever happy.

The people at the school were so nice to me. The principal was nice. Mr. Long, however, said he wanted me to agree to something. He wanted me to understand that I could not ask off for a funeral or wedding or to go to any professional meeting because he was hiring me to be a teacher, not a pastor. The principal told me she had to follow Mr. Long's objectives, but if I had to leave early, she would do her best to work with me. I told the board of deacons that if a funeral was needed, it would have to begin at 3:30; they didn't like it. I would be speeding trying to get to these events at the church, and sometimes I would be five to ten minutes late. I was so upset.

The person who removed me from this dilemma was my wife, Bertie. She knew how upset I was and said, "Grady, don't sign a contract for next year with the school board. I'll try to get a job teaching." She was certified to teach English and French, but there were no vacancies in Richmond. She was offered a teaching job at A. G. Richardson High School in Louisa, Virginia, and she said to me, "I'll take the job and you just give up teaching and be the pastor that you want to be!" She drove forty-six miles one way to get there, ninety-two miles a day, so that this family of four could make it, and we did it. I was so grateful to Bertie for what she had done! This, I can never forget.

I stayed at Quioccasin for three years and was able to immerse myself in the work of the church and the community. I joined several community organizations, such as the Richmond Citizens Advisory Committee (RCAC), the local NAACP, and the Baptist General Convention, as well as the Virginia Council of Churches and many others. Quioccasin was where I really launched my life as a pastor and community participant.

PART V

Afternoon

Chapter Eight

From Quioccasin to Gillfield

Life's sun was shining brightly with its full spectrum. My life seemed like a series of images formed from radiant energy that brought a focus, a sense of direction for which I had longed.

In 1961, I was called to Gillfield Baptist Church in Petersburg, Virginia, the third oldest African American congregation in the nation. Gillfield was 164 years old, and I was just twenty-eight. By this time, we had three children. When we finished Virginia Union, Bertie was carrying Grady Jr. as she walked across the stage for graduation. When I came to Petersburg, Grady Jr. was eighteen months old, Dot was four, and Sandra was six.

There were three men who were very influential in my coming to Gillfield. One was Dr. John Malcus Ellison. After meeting Dr. Ellison that day when I rang the doorbell at the wrong house, he became my mentor. I came to Virginia Union, where he had been the first black president, and I entered the seminary. While I was there, Dr. Ellison always did what he could to elevate my status. Another person was Dr. Allix P. James. Dr. James was dean of the seminary. He taught two courses that enriched my perspective of the pastorate—Church Worship and Church Administration. He took special interest in me and encouraged me to consider serving just one church. (As a very significant note, Dr. James and I transcended the relationship of teacher and student long ago, and today he is my personal friend.) The other person who was involved in my becoming pastor at Gillfield Baptist Church was a godly old man by the name of Deacon Henry Clifton Patrick Burke.

Gillfield was looking for a pastor in 1961 and Deacon Burke was on the search committee. He was very familiar with Virginia Union University and went to Dr. Ellison and asked him for some recommendations. Dr. Ellison recommended three preachers. One day, I was at the Ministers Conference and a lady named Miss Maria Burke, who was secretary at Ebenezer, came down and gave me a little note saying, "There's a man Deacon Burke from Petersburg upstairs. He wants to see you." So I went upstairs. He said, "I'm H. C. P. Burke. I'm a deacon at Gillfield, Baptist Church in Petersburg, Virginia. Rev. Powell, we've been told that you might consider our church. Would you come to preach for us?" "Yes sir, I will come," I replied.

I got a date to preach and carried out the engagement. Bertie did not come with me, but I left Gillfield feeling ok. That's all. Two weeks later, they called me and asked if I would come back. They said, "Would you bring your wife this time and also serve communion for us?" Communion was at night. Finally he stated, "And you can have dinner with us." So I came over and I brought my wife and children, and we had dinner. We were coming down Wilcox St. and he said, "Reverend, I want to show you something." He said, "That's the parsonage."

Something strange happened. Deacon Burke told me that they were very interested in me, but they were not going to call a pastor until April or May. Deacon Burke later told me the search committee was pushing him for a decision in March! The members were fussing with the pulpit committee because they weren't doing this and that. The committee asked him, "You don't have anybody to recommend?" Deacon Burke replied, "We have one but we haven't finished checking on him." "Well who is it?" they asked. "Rev. Grady W. Powell," he answered, and they voted me in right there. I knew nothing about it. I was in Richmond at Quioccasin, and the church was building a parsonage, a beautiful split-level home. I was going to take a wife and three children into this new home on a half acre of land. I could not leave Quioccasin Church.

One night in March, the telephone rang. I was in the kitchen getting a glass of milk. "Hello, Rev. Powell. This is Deacon Burke of Gillfield. I want you to know that because of the church's situation, we called someone tonight and I thought I should let you know." I said, "All right, Deacon Burke." He said, "Don't you want to know who we called?" I said, "It would be nice to know." He said, "We called a Rev. Grady W. Powell from Richmond, Virginia!" Lord, it made me nervous. He said, "What do you think of that?" I said, "Fine, but I'll let you know." I went to tell Bertie, and she went into a cry. She said, "Grady, I told you to tell those people you weren't coming. Quioccasin is building a house for us and they are such kind people." I said, "Bertie, I don't know. I don't know."

I called Henry Townes, who was my best friend in the world. He was in Covington, Virginia. I said, "Henry, I've got something to tell you. I don't know what to do." I told him that the next morning I was going to talk to Dr. James and Dr. Ellison about whether I should go to Gillfield or stay at Quioccasin. I was going to tell them I didn't think I could go to Gillfield, even though they'd recommended me and the church was interested. "Henry, what should I do? Everything is so confusing." He said, "Now listen, Grady. That might be God getting ahead of you, and don't get in the way of God. Grady, you just think about it." So the next day, I went to Dr. James's office and said, "Dr. James, I want to talk to you about Gillfield, but it's altogether new. I had some questions about what to do, but you know they called me last night." Dr. James said, "What! They didn't tell us, but Grady, you ought to go. It's a scholarly church. You are a scholarly man. You would do well at that church. You can lead them." He convinced me I ought to seriously consider the call.

So I called another close friend, Deacon William Lewis, a member of Quioccasin. He came to see me. He said, "Rev. Powell, don't you tell Quioccasin I told you this, but you ought to leave us. I tell you just like I would tell my son. That church will be able to pay you more than we can pay you, and Reverend, you have an up-and-coming family. You are an up-and-coming pastor and you ought to go, but don't tell them I said it."

The men of Quioccasin got wind of what was going on and found out Gillfield was offering me $5,200 per year with a parsonage. Now Quioccasin was building a parsonage and a group of men at Quioccasin approached me and said they would pay me for the rest of the year enough so that I would get $5,200, $100 per week. When December came, they said, they would vote that the church pay me by the budget and that would be just as much as Gillfield was paying.

William Lewis came down to my house to talk to me. He said, "Reverend, that's nice, but don't take it. Gillfield is starting you at $5,200. We would be stretching ourselves to give you the same. Each year, Gillfield will be carrying you upward in pay and I don't know if we could do that." So I weighed all the advice from my family, friends, and confidants. I took the job as pastor of Gillfield and resigned the pastorate at Quioccasin.

So on June 24, 1961, I preached my first Sunday at Gillfield. I looked out at the congregation from the pulpit and who was in the audience . . . ? William Lewis.

We moved to Petersburg on Friday, June 23, 1961. We didn't have much furniture at that time, so we got all of it in the house that day. Afterwards, we decided to go down to Brunswick County and spend the night with Mama and Dad. We would come back the next morning and put up at least the beds and get started setting up the house.

I wish I could remember the name of the company that moved us to Petersburg, because they were a black-owned company. They charged us $75. I was not familiar with what it meant to be a CEO of a church. I learned later that I should have asked Gillfield to move me. They should have paid the $75, but I didn't know it.

On Saturday morning we were back in Petersburg. Mrs. Greene, who was the wife of the chairman of the deacon board, told us she would have us over for dinner. That enabled us to work all day long on Saturday morning and early afternoon. We went to the Greenes' about 4:00 and had dinner. We brought our eighteen-month-old baby and put him down on the floor to sleep while the two girls, my wife, and I ate dinner. We came back home to 312 S. Dunlop Street, and continued to set up things Saturday night. Finally, we went to bed.

I got up the next morning, June 24, 1961, to go to Gillfield to preach my first sermon as a resident pastor. As previously mentioned, it was good to see Bill Lewis from Quioccasin in the audience. It was a tough decision to leave Quioccasin and his support was vital to me. That was quite an historic day for me. I don't know why, but I can't remember the sermon I preached that day. Obviously, it wasn't that significant. But I do remember how the people welcomed me. That day they had a reception right after worship for me. We have a picture of it: Bertie, the children, Deacon and Mrs. Greene. We all stood in a line after church and they served some cookies and punch. People came by and shook my hand. I was pleased and, finally, so was my wife.

We didn't have any food in the house yet, so I asked about a restaurant where we could go for dinner. There was no restaurant in town we could go to because of strict segregation, but Miss Sadie Roberts of Gillfield told me about a restaurant on 460 Highway East that was owned and operated by blacks. The restaurant was named Forest View and we had dinner there: my wife, my three children, and myself. It was a nice place, a gathering place for blacks. Mr. T. O. Thweatt, the owner, was a great leader in civil rights and social justice. Some called him a radical. Our meeting that Sunday afternoon was mutually meaningful.

I asked Deacon Greene and Deacon Burke if on that Monday, my first day in office, would they take me around to see the people who were sick and shut in. That was the best move I had ever made as a pastor. They were so impressed that I would visit the sick the first day I was on the job. We visited Mrs. Virgie Sparks, who owned Wilkerson's Funeral Home. We visited Ms. Ida Jackson. She was a Perry, the sister to the treasurer of the church. We visited six to eight people who were shut in. I wish I could remember all the people we visited that day. When we returned to the church in the early afternoon, Deacon Greene and Deacon Burke realized that they had forgotten the key.

I was struck by the fact that when we arrived at the church, there was a big crowd near the church. I asked the deacons what was going on. They didn't know, so I said, "Well, I'm going to find out." I found out that on that very day they were auctioning off twelve pieces of property right next door to the church and nobody from the church had apprised himself of it. We should have been involved in this purchase of land. The selling price was $3,000, and Gillfield could have paid that so easily. It would take us four years to buy the property that sold for $3,000 that day. When we purchased it four years later, we paid $12,000 for it. I decided from that point on, I would be on top of everything in Petersburg that had any kind of connection with Gillfield Church.

I remember the very first meeting I had with the executive committee. The committee consisted of Walker Quarles, Cordlandt Colson, and William Greene. The official board asked them to meet with me and negotiate salary and other matters. I knew they were going to pay me $5,200 per year. That's what they told me before I was called. I was very grateful for this amount. I also wanted a discretionary fund that I could use for small missions such as when, for example, I wanted to give five dollars to someone in need of a meal. I explained that this was the type of pastor I had been and wanted to continue to be. So, the church gave me twenty-five dollars per month to use at my discretion. They also agreed to give the Easter, Thanksgiving, and Christmas offerings in this manner. If persons came by the church and needed some money, I could appraise their worthiness. I would report this spending to the chairman, vice chairman, and secretary of the deacon board. The reason I wanted to submit that report was because I didn't want people to think I was using the money for personal use.

Sometimes a college student would come by and need three to five dollars for, say, a prescription to be filled. I would let them know the church was handling this and then write a check to a particular agency, like a drug store. Writing a check would enable the committee to see the payment and to whom it had gone. The total of the three special offerings and the twenty-five dollars per week being put in the pastor's fund might add up to $1,000 or more. So sometimes when a child wanted to get into college and needed $150 or so, I could write a check. Sometimes when the death of a person occurred, the family would say, in lieu of flowers, give to the Gillfield Church Pastor's Fund. I never wrote a check to myself and I never wrote a check to any of my children or my wife.

So with this fund I was able to do a lot of things that allowed the influence of Gillfield Church to penetrate the Petersburg community. If something was happening in the city, like the building of the YMCA, I could give $200 to the YMCA and they would think, "That's a wonderful thing Gillfield is doing!" I didn't have to go to the church or have any kind of board meetings for approval. I would do quarterly reports to the committees and that was that. It was a missions fund and it worked out very well. When it was time for me to retire, I asked that the record book on discretionary spending be sealed, because I didn't want people's personal information to become public. I believe that book is at the church in the safe deposit box to this day.

The church also paid for my telephone, fuel, water bill, and lights at the parsonage. But I had heard some members complaining about past expenses with respect to utilities. I understood why lights were on. It was for safety. The previous pastor, Rev. Wyatt T. Walker, had been so involved with Martin Luther King, Jr., and civil rights that there was always the threat of violence with Wyatt getting home so late. I knew that my wife also had some frights about being home alone and she would leave lights on too, and I would want that for her.

So, I thought a better way for them to do this would be to come up with a budget for these four bills and just give it to me. We settled on $300 for the year, and they just gave it to me in a lump sum. That was an adequate amount, and if I was frugal enough, I would have some money left. If I overspent, I would take care of it out of my salary. We worked all of that out to everyone's satisfaction. So I had a livable wage salary, a parsonage in which to live, and money for the necessary fees that were related to household expenses.

I discussed some other things with the executive committee about my job responsibilities and what they expected from me. I said to them, "You expect every pastor to bless the babies, preach on Sunday, bury the dead, etc. Those routine things are understood, but what else do you want me to accomplish outside of the normal tasks pastors take on?"

They replied that they wanted me to lead them in building a Christian Education Center. I began to talk about it, but I was soon convinced that talking about the Christian Education Center was not the proper thing. I decided I would talk about the acquisition of property, because we had no property on which to build. There was some space in the back, enough to park about six to eight cars, but that wasn't big enough to build a building.

Walker Quarles, who later became Dr. Quarles, was chairman of the trustee board. I talked to Walker and the trustee board about the acquisition of property. I remember I pushed them to get the corner piece of property. There was a little pink building on the corner and I knew if we got that piece, we could block anyone else from getting property on Gill Street or on Perry Street down by the church.

It took some time, but I must say that Dr. Walker Quarles really worked with me and was a tremendous help in moving the process forward. Whenever a person accomplishes something great, he or she never does it alone. A family named Scott in Amelia owned that little pink house on the corner and through an attorney, we were able to acquire it. That was the beginning of the physical expansion of Gillfield Baptist Church. As I remember, we got that in the early part of 1962. In the end, Gillfield purchased twenty-four pieces of property, where the church now has a Christian Education Center.

Gillfield was a wonderful place to work because of dedicated Christian people from different educational levels. We had a lot of people from Virginia State and many who worked in the public schools: Dinwiddie, Prince George, and Petersburg. We also had several persons who were laborers. We had individuals who owned businesses: the Griffins owned a shoe store; the Sparks owned a funeral home; Deacon Burke, who was chairman of the search committee that called me as pastor, had a wonderful paper hanging business; the chair of the deacon board was Deacon Greene, who was one of the best builders Petersburg ever had. Deacon Greene was also head of building and grounds for Virginia State. Some persons thought that everybody was highly educated at Gillfield, but I knew of a member who could not read or write. There were many people who had not finished elementary school.

There was something very unique about the founders of Gillfield. Gillfield Baptist Church was founded by free blacks who had never been slaves. The church started out in Prince George County under the name of Davenport Church, but there were white people in the church. There were Native Americans in the church and free blacks—free blacks who had come to America looking for their fortune. It was in 1797 that the church had been founded. Because there was so much industry in Petersburg at that time, particularly in a section called Pocahontas, the blacks in the Davenport Church decided that they wanted to move to Petersburg. The other members didn't want to move, so the blacks came to Petersburg in 1797 and built a small building on the Appomattox River that they called the Sandy Beach Church. In 1818, because of flooding conditions, they moved to Collier's Alley and they changed the name to the Church of the Lord Jesus Christ of Petersburg.

In 1821, they purchased some property from George Pillsboro. It was purchased out of the Gillfield plat, which had been owned by Erasmus Gill. Gill was a good friend to Peter Jones, one of the founders of Petersburg, and they bought a plat of land from George Pillsboro and named it "Gillfield." That was in 1821, and since 1821, that congregation has been known as Gillfield. That's some of the history for the church that I was privileged to serve for almost thirty-seven years.

Gillfield was very open to me as a pastor who believed in liturgical settings of services. So I was privileged to work with people who had some rather interesting and high ideals about the order of worship service. The organist was a woman named Mildred Brown Williams. She was the daughter of Rev. Samuel A. Brown, the longest-serving pastor in the history of Gillfield Baptist Church. He served for thirty-nine years. I talked to Mrs. Williams about worship and she was open to my ideas. We talked about the hymns that would be played on Sunday and things such as printing the preludes for the educational purposes of the congregation. Education was high on her interest list because she was the black supervisor of education in Dinwiddie County.

When I came to Gillfield, Mrs. Williams was playing one song for the prelude. It was a wonderful song entitled "Through a Cathedral Window." I began to talk to her about other hymns and preludes, and she began to play them on Sunday. I would always call her at her office in Dinwiddie and she would approve them. She would in turn tell me what she wanted to play, and I would approve her selections and that was that. We worked very well together. I wanted to begin to print in the bulletin even the scripture we were going to read. I always printed the subject of the sermon, every Sunday for thirty-six years. I only changed it once, when Jack Kennedy was shot, because I wanted to share in the sadness of the nation. Sometimes, it is far better, in terms of the spirit of the church, to have a great person as your partner than to have a great professional. Mrs. Williams was not a professional musician, but she was indeed a great person.

The professional musician I worked with was Mrs. Altoona Johns, Dr. Vernon John's wife. She only played for the Sunday school. One of the songs she frequently played was "Jesu, Joy of Man's Desiring," one of my all-time favorites. Dr. Johns was the pastor who paved the way for Dr. Martin L. King, Jr., at Dexter Avenue Baptist Church. He was a true trailblazer. A made-for-TV movie was completed on the life on Vernon Johns and was filmed in Petersburg. Ironically, many scenes were filmed at Gillfield Baptist Church.

We did not have a choir director in my early years at Gillfield. I always considered myself a frustrated choir director. I love to sing and direct music, but I never thought it was appropriate for the pastor to be a soloist. But what I would do was lead congregational singing. I knew that in the audience were professional musicians: Mrs. Hazel Stone Rainey, who finished Virginia State in music; Marion Spikes, who finished Knoxville College in Tennessee, as well as her sister, Miss Esther Franklin; Dr. F. Nathaniel Gatlin, who headed the music department at Virginia State; and the distinguished Dr. Undine Smith Moore, who was one of the most accomplished African American composers in the United States.

One Sunday, I directed congregational singing on "Great Is Thy Faithfulness." I had the congregation singing the song in its full musical splendor. After worship, I wanted to see what Dr. Moore thought about it. As I was shaking members' hands at the door, she approached. I said, "Dr. Moore, how did I do?" She said, "Well, you certainly have volume!" and went on her way. Those were the good old days, and we built up worship, and the congregation built up an appreciation of the same. The professional musicians were supportive, especially Dr. F. Nathaniel Gatlin, who was a deacon.

In 1963, our fourth child was born. I remember the anticipation surrounding the birth of Herbert. The congregation was excited that the pastor and his wife were going to have a Petersburg baby. Herbert was born at the end of July, a time when I would normally have been on vacation in Pittsburgh with my in-laws. But that summer when Herbert was to be born, we couldn't leave. What could we do for a vacation? I normally took a month off for vacation, and I needed it. When I returned, I would feel so refreshed and ready to go.

I mentioned my vacation dilemma to my pastor in Brunswick County, Rev. W. H. Winston. He told me about a lady in Lunenburg County who lived alone and was the finest cook this side of heaven. He said she also had a nice comfortable home, loved to take people in and she would charge visitors whatever they wanted to pay. He gave me her name and number. Her name was Mrs. Morrison.

So my family and I went to Mrs. Morrison's home in Lunenburg County. She made the most special rolls. I'll never forget them as long as I live. That was a wonderful time. She was a great cook. We just walked around the yard. There was a tobacco farm nearby, where I helped gather the tobacco, a task familiar to me. I also helped pick beans. Both activities renewed my spirit.

We returned to Petersburg on July 15 because of the impending birth. On July 28, my wife went to the hospital, which at that time was called Petersburg General Hospital. On the morning of July 29, the doctor told me, "You have another boy!" Never in my life had I prayed so hard for a boy, because I had two girls and they grew up so nicely together. I wanted another boy to grow up with Grady Jr. I was so happy.

Grady Powell, Sr., age 17
High school senior portrait

His mother, Lillie

Grady with daughter Sandra at
Quioccasin Baptist Church office, 1958

His daughters' double wedding, which was held at Gillfield Baptist Church in 1981 (photo taken at family home)

His wife, Bertie

With his sisters, from left to right: Mable, Grady, and Irene

With his brothers and father, from left to right: Grady, Charlie, Percy, Herbert (father), and Mert

Time with the children at St. James Baptist Church

Grady preaching at the pulpit

Gillfield Baptist Church, where Grady served as pastor for 36 years

Grady's entire immediate family at Garland Avenue Baptist Church.
Top row, left to right: Albert, Herb, Grady Jr., Grady III, Harvey III
Bottom row, left to right: Danette, Harvey, Dot, Bertie, Eric, Sandra,
Grady Sr.

Sharing the rostrum with Mrs. Doris Piercy at Gillfield Baptist
Church on Brown & Williamson Day

Speaking about the heritage of Justice Cleo Powell at the Virginia Supreme Court

Featured on the cover of the American
Baptist Churches USA magazine

CHAPTER NINE

Civil Rights in Petersburg

Gillfield Baptist Church had a noble history. My predecessor, Rev. Wyatt T. Walker, did the finest job. His main task, one that was most needed at that time, was civil rights and social justice, and he gave most of his time to that. Rev. Walker was so effective in this area that Martin Luther King, Jr., hired him to be the executive director of the Southern Christian Leadership Conference. Wyatt had been arrested, for an example, for refusing to sit in the black section at the Petersburg Public Library. The black section was in the basement and he refused to go down there. They threw him in jail.

Gillfield in those early days presented a wonderful challenge to me. It was a challenge of the community. I had to be very, very careful how I worked because some of the people, the older people in particular, had become very discouraged and disenchanted with Rev. Walker because he was so active in civil rights and had made Gillfield a kind of center for civil rights. But I knew that Rev. Walker was right. So I worked to get Gillfield committed, and I'm happy to say that Gillfield Baptist Church was a church most committed to civil rights and social justice in my early days there. I was able to convince them that the path Wyatt started was the path to be on.

I walked right into a continuation of Wyatt's civil rights struggle. People threw eggs at my door. I received threatening telephone calls in the middle of the night with people just breathing on the other end of the line. Once, a cross was burned in front of Gillfield while we were in revival. I will never forget it. Dr. Margaret Crowder was leaving revival early that night in order to take her daughter home and go the hospital where she worked. She walked outside and saw a cross burning on our lot! She ran in and told Tyree Felder, who was ushering that night. He rushed up to me with a little note that said, "Cross is being burned outside!" We were singing at the time and I announced, "Hold it! There's a cross being burned outside. Let's go out and look at it." We went out and there was a cross standing about five feet tall that was set up against the church. Thank God the church was made of brick so it did not catch fire. It was the work of the KKK. They had a cell that met monthly in an Ettrick restaurant. So we called the police and they came over. They conducted an investigation. I still have a copy of the newspaper article that was published in the Afro-American newspaper on April 20, 1963. It read in part as follows:

> A Hanover County man was charged with burning a cross in front of Gillfield Baptist Church Tuesday night where a revival service was being held. Guest speaker was the Rev. C. L. Evans. The church is pastored by the Rev. Grady Powell, a courageous young man who succeeded Rev. Wyatt T. Walker, who is now executive director of the SCLC. Rev. Powell said he did not feel the incident was an expression of the majority of the white race, but a minority of the white race. Rev. Powell asked the police chief if he could keep the cross as a souvenir for future generations and the captain gladly did. The cross was about five and one-half feet high wrapped in oil soaked rags. Several witnesses in the predominantly colored residential area saw a car drive off with five white men. The chief of police identified the suspect as James Ben Rowe, 34, of Rte. 3, Ellerson . . .

In the midst of these difficulties, I was also able to give time to Gillfield's pastoral ministry. I had regular pastoral visitation, met with the Sunday school teachers weekly, and was involved with the church music and hymn selection. I did it by the book of involving people in Christian education and in church administration, but also in civil rights and social justice. I think that method convinced them.

As pastor of Gillfield, I became a member of one of the most important committees that helped to change race relations in Petersburg. It was called the Bi-Racial Committee, and on that committee were six persons: three blacks and three whites. The blacks were Hermanze Fauntleroy, Robert Cooley, and myself. The whites were Lewis Shell, Bay Jacobs, and Lester Bowman. Gillfield was very proud of my being on that committee and that's why I knew they were committed to civil rights and social justice. We negotiated opening up every restaurant, the theater, and every public place to all races. We negotiated that and all of us signed the manifesto, except Lester Bowman. The very day we signed the manifesto, the Supreme Court issued its decision, on December 12, 1964. This case was entitled *Heart of Atlanta Motel, Inc. v. United States* and the report of the case reads as follows (as reported in Wikipedia):

> The Civil Rights Act of 1964 prohibited places of "public accommodation" from discrimination based on customers' race, sex, color, religion, or national origin. The Heart of Atlanta Motel challenged the constitutionality of this provision and, after losing before a three-judge federal court, appealed to the Supreme Court.
>
> The Supreme Court ruled that Congress had the power under the Commerce Clause to enact the prohibitions on discrimination contained in the public accommodations section of the Civil Rights Act of 1964. Justice Thomas Clark wrote the opinion for a unanimous Court. He reviewed testimony presented at congressional hearings showing that Americans had become increasingly mobile, but that African Americans were discriminated against by hotels and motels, and often had to travel longer distances to get lodging or had to call on friends to put them up overnight.
>
> Justice Clark noted that under the Interstate Commerce Act, " . . . The power of Congress to promote interstate commerce also includes the power to regulate the local incidents thereof, including local activities in both the States of origin and destination, which might have a substantial and harmful effect upon that commerce. One need only examine the evidence which we have discussed above to see that Congress may—as it has—prohibit racial discrimination by motels serving travelers, however 'local' their operations may appear."

Justice Clark also found that the Act did not deprive the motel owner of liberty or property under the Fifth Amendment. Because Congress has the right to prohibit discrimination in accommodations under the Interstate Commerce Act, the motel "has no 'right' to select its guests as it sees fit, free from government regulation."

Their decision was right in line with our manifesto. Unfortunately, all five of those persons are dead now, and I'm the only one alive.

Lester Bowman adamantly opposed that manifesto and made his opposition known to the committee by stating that if any restaurant wanted to say that only a certain type of person could come in and eat, that the owner of business had the right to say that. If the owner said only baldheaded men could come in and eat, that was his right. Freedom in America. That was Lester Bowman's thing. But the two other whites signed the manifesto, and there were a lot of whites who agreed with them. We owe Lewis Shell and Alexander Bay Jacobs a tremendous amount of gratitude. It may sound small now, but it was a big step for them to take at the time. They were vilified by many, while Lester Bowman was praised as a person who believed in the rights and freedoms of citizens.

Lewis Shell was a member of the largest law firm in Petersburg, and I don't know how his partners felt about his civil rights involvement, but obviously they agreed with him or just accepted his beliefs. He was with the law firm of White, Hamilton, Wyche and Shell, where he went right after law school. I was proud of him because what he did could have been very upsetting to that law firm, but it didn't seem to have affected it.

Bay Jacobs owned a shoe store in downtown Petersburg. I think it was called Jacobs Shoe Store. I was proud of Bay Jacobs, who was Jewish. He signed the manifesto, but his action did not cause his store to close. There were some who stopped going to his store, but most kept going.

Lester Bowman made a statement in the paper, and because he was so adamant about what the Bi-Racial Committee had done, he had a write-in candidacy to city council and he was elected.

Gillfield backed me up while I was on that committee, for which I was most pleased. Another time I was shown that Gillfield was committed to civil rights and social justice was during the Selma to Montgomery March with Dr. King. At a meeting, I told the official board how important the march was and suggested we have a prayer for the marchers at prayer meeting that Wednesday night. Dr. Cordlandt Colson said, "Rev. Powell, do you want to go?" I said, "I would love to go!" He said, "I move that the church would send Rev. Powell to the Selma to Montgomery March!" And so it was that Gillfield Baptist Church sent me to the Selma to Montgomery March. They were going to pay for me to fly down there. That was the opportunity of a lifetime!

I tried to get a ticket to fly into Montgomery, but I couldn't. Every plane, every train was booked solid. I didn't want to take the bus. It would take too long. I called my good friend, Rev. John Cross, Jr., who was my classmate in the seminary at Virginia Union. John was the pastor of Sixteenth Street Baptist Church in Birmingham, Alabama, when it was bombed on September 15, 1963, and four little girls were killed. That bombing marked a turning point in the Civil Rights Movement.

John suggested that I fly into Birmingham because they were going to go to the march the next morning. People were encouraged to meet the march five miles outside of Montgomery and march all the way with King into the city. I flew into Birmingham. John met me at the airport and drove me to his house. What an experience that was—it felt like a war zone! I thought Petersburg was tough in terms of racism, but it was nothing compared to Birmingham.

When John and I arrived at his home, he told me that the guest bedroom at the front of the house was very vulnerable to KKK attacks, and gave me three instructions: (1) *Don't get in bed on the side near the picture window. Get in bed on the other side so people won't see your shadow.* (2) *If you can, put the light out so that no one can shoot through the window.* (3) *If you hear any noise around the house, don't get up. Just roll over and quietly get under the bed. If you get up, somebody can shoot you.*

Such was the state of civil rights and social justice in Birmingham, Alabama, 1965.

The next morning, John and I got up at 3:00 A.M. in order to catch up with the march. We went out first in the dark with his flashlight and looked around the house. He said, "We are taught just to check because people have been ambushed and killed." Next he lay down on one of those platforms that mechanics lie on to roll under cars. He slid under his car to see if any bombs had been attached during the night. He said, "We have to look for safety purposes." John continued with his list of precautions and warnings by saying, "Never look threatening to any car that may come up in front of you, behind you, or beside you, because someone may shoot you." It really frightened me!

Although somewhat afraid, I felt exhilarated with positive thoughts. First, I was in the march with leaders of this nation, representing such groups as the National Council of Churches, American Baptist Churches, the National Baptist Convention, United Methodist Churches, Protestant Episcopal Churches, Roman Catholic Churches and many others. Second, I knew I was not only on the right side of history but the winning side as well.

In April of 1875, the last shot was fired in the Civil War, a war that was fought over slavery. One hundred years later, on March 16, 1965, we began the Selma to Montgomery March. The cause for freedom continues worldwide, as we have witnessed in the Middle East uprisings in Egypt, Libya, and now in Syria. All over the world, people keep marching for freedom, one step at a time.

All we wanted was the right to vote, and so we marched, one foot after the other, one step at a time, for civil rights and social justice. From memory and news reports, the weather that day was clear. All I could see was a sea of people. There were people to my right and left as well as people in front and in back of me. Everyone was joined together by a common purpose: freedom and equality. We walked along U.S. Route 80, known in Alabama as the Jefferson Davis Highway. We were protected by 2,000 U.S. Army soldiers and 1,900 members of the Alabama National Guard under federal command. The group reached Montgomery on March 24, 1965, and we all arrived on March 25 at the Alabama State Capitol. The route is memorialized as the Selma to Montgomery Voting Rights Trail, a National Historic Trail.

My good friend Rev. John Cross was a true civil rights warrior and he will always be remembered in America as the pastor of Sixteenth Street Baptist Church when it was bombed and those little girls were killed. He passed away in 2007 at the age of eighty-two.

I remember being on that plane coming back from the Selma to Montgomery March and reflecting on all that I had seen there. Thinking now of those days gone by, my mind drifts back to my beginnings in civil rights.

Chapter Ten

Civil Rights Connections from Earlier Days

Like the book of Genesis, I ought to include a statement that tells how "stuff" began. The book of Genesis simply says, "In the beginning God . . . " So I have asked myself, How did I become interested in civil rights? "Grady, in the beginning what?" I've asked myself. I believe I would say, "In the beginning, my father . . . "

Though my father would never be registered as a civil rights leader, upon reflection, I see that he truly was. He was a local leader when I was in my early teens. In 1947, he became the first black person in the Powellton district, Butlers precinct, of Brunswick County to register to vote since 1874, during Reconstruction. He said he didn't have a problem with registering because there was a blank paper registration then and he took his "pony" with him. He pulled it out so he could copy it. My father didn't write fast or very well. He said he was still writing the information down when the registrar, a man named Mitchell, came into the room. Mitchell addressed him with the name the local white folks used for him, asking, "Uncle Herbert, are you finished?" Daddy replied, "Go back, I haven't finished yet!"

After he had registered, Daddy started talking about how other people needed to register to vote. I heard him talking with a man named Haywood A. Reavis about registering to vote. Mr. Reavis had been one of the early graduates of Virginia Normal and Industrial Institute, which is now Virginia State University. He returned to Brunswick County. He was also a member of Poplar Mount Baptist Church and so was my father. In fact, my father was a deacon. I was told by my mother that when she went to kneel down by my daddy when the deacons were going to lay their hands on them for his deacon ordination, she was pregnant with me and she felt me kick inside her. That was 1932. Anyway, Daddy had been a deacon for about twelve to fourteen years, and he talked with Haywood Reavis about registering to vote. Mr. Reavis went to register.

Daddy would stand up in Sunday school and say, "If you don't register and vote, you ain't no citizen!" Of course he was technically incorrect, but he was correct in terms of sharing the responsibility of citizenship. I heard my father at the Sunday School Union talk about the importance of voting. The Sunday School Union, Bethesda, was a group of about twenty to twenty-five Sunday schools in joint session. This group met every fifth Sunday. I would hear him talk about Harry Byrd. He would say, "We will pull the feathers out of the tail of that bird!" I didn't know much about all this at the time. I was about thirteen years old. But if I ask myself now how it all started, I would have to say with my father. Civil rights and social justice for me began with him.

My father would also say to us, "Don't work for the white man. Work for yourself." He didn't see school teaching as working for the white man because it took place in a black school. He didn't realize the schoolteachers got their salary through the actions of white folks. So, he wanted his own farm and that's what he did. He told us stories about my grandfather, Jim Powell, who was freed as a slave when he was twelve years old. He told us stories about how a potential riot arose at Ante Store because a white man had treated a black man wrong and the black man broke a chair over his head. He talked about many race-related subjects in and out of the house, and upon reflection, I really think that's how I became interested in civil rights.

The second phase of my civil rights education began with a man named E. D. Adkins. Edward D. Atkins was a native of Mississippi, so I learned many years later. He lived in Brunswick County and he taught me at Saint Paul's High School. One must remember that there were no public schools for blacks when I was of high school age. Saint Paul's College provided the high school. My understanding was that the county gave them money, but it wasn't one-half of what was given to whites. So Saint Paul's College established a high school, and that's where I encountered Mr. Adkins in 1946. The great thing about Mr. Adkins was that every week he made us learn something about our history. We had to know the national Negro hymn, "Lift Every Voice and Sing," by James Weldon Johnson. I can still sing every word of it today from memory. In Mr. Adkins's class, we were also expected to know the preamble to the Constitution, Lincoln's Gettysburg Address, and many others.

Mr. Adkins talked with us about Sojourner Truth. He talked about Benjamin Banneker and joked that if you go to Washington, D.C., and get lost, blame it on a black man, because he laid out the design for the city. He knew Carter G. Woodson and talked about him frequently.

The biggest thing Mr. Adkins did was to make a pact with his students, and it was this: for every person that you get to register to vote, I will add an "A" to the grades that you have. Honestly, I didn't know at that time the implications of registering and voting. I did understand, however, the implications of getting an "A," and I set out to get people to register to vote.

The first person I got to register to vote was my brother. He served in World War II and was in high school with me. I was one grade ahead of him. His name was Mercy Vermont Powell. We called him Mert. I talked with Mert about registering. We had what was known as the blank paper registration, and Mr. Adkins had written down everything we needed to know. First, you would write the date, day and year at the top. You would then write "My name is Mercy V. Powell. I was born in Brunswick County, Virginia." And then you would put your date of birth and so forth.

Mert and I practiced the voter registration requirements every day when we would come home. I actually had him take a blank piece of paper and practice all twenty-one lines and I knew after a while, he had it. So we rode together by bus to the registrar's location, which was at Ante Store. The registrar was William Mitchell, the same man who registered my father. The two of them went into the back of the store, where they keep the fertilizer. What a place to register to vote, huh? There was a little table back there and Mert began the process. I could not stay in there with him, so Mr. Mitchell sent me out to sit on the steps of the store.

When the door opened and Mert emerged, I was elated. We had worked so hard on this. I said, "Mert, you're registered!" He said, "But I didn't pass Grady. I didn't pass!" My heart sank. "You didn't pass Mert?" I replied. "Nah, Grady, I didn't," he responded in a rather sad tone. He had worked so hard in preparation. I asked, "Why didn't you pass?" He started unfolding a piece of paper and said, "You didn't tell me about this word I was supposed to know. Here, I wrote it down." It said "folio." I didn't know what a folio was! Mr. Adkins had not told me about knowing such a word!

So the next morning we took the bus to Saint Paul's campus in a dash to see Mr. Adkins. We literally ran up the stairs to the third or fourth floor of Webster Hall to Mr. Adkins's room, and I burst through the door. "Mr. Adkins!" I exclaimed. "Here is my brother Mert and he didn't pass!" He replied, "Did you fill out all the required spaces, Mert?" "I did!" Mert stated anxiously. Mr. Adkins pondered and asked, "Well, why didn't you pass?" I said, "Mr. Mitchell asked him a question after he finished the written requirement. He asked him the meaning of the word 'folio.'" Mr. Adkins said in astonishment, "Folio!" An angry yet determined look came over Mr. Adkins's face and he said, "Ok. I want both of you to wait for me after school and I'm going to take you in my car to see Mr. Mitchell. We will find out what he's doing!"

Well, I felt happy knowing that something was wrong. I had done what I was supposed to do to get an "A" and Mr. Adkins knew it. That afternoon, we didn't get on Warner's bus. We told Warner we would be riding with Mr. Adkins, and people started wondering why Mr. Adkins was going to see Mr. Mitchell. So Mr. Adkins drove what I guess was probably over ten or twelve miles to Ante Store. That's the kind of teacher we had in Mr. Adkins. He was doing this for us off the clock and unpaid. He believed in the cause of civil rights.

When we arrived at the store, Mr. Mitchell was out back milking cows. We went to him and Mr. Adkins did an unthinkable thing. He addressed himself as "Mr." He said, "Mr. Mitchell, I'm Mr. Adkins." Mr. Mitchell looked back over his shoulder and said, "Yes, Mr. Adkins?" Well, I was shocked right off the bat because white men never addressed black men as "Mister." Mr. Adkins stated, "Mr. Mitchell, I understand this young man came to you to register yesterday." Mr. Mitchell replied, "Yeah, he did." Mr. Adkins continued, "I understand he didn't pass." "Naw, he didn't," Mr. Mitchell responded. "And why didn't he pass?" was Mr. Mitchell's swift response. "There was some word Mert didn't know," Mr. Mitchell answered. "What word didn't he know, Mr. Mitchell?" Mr. Adkins asked. "I don't remember, Mr. Adkins. I just have a dictionary in there and I just opened it to any page and I saw that word and it looked like a nice word. I had never seen it before. We were told as a registrar, we could use any word we wanted or anything we wanted and if they didn't know it, they couldn't pass," Mr. Mitchell explained.

Mr. Adkins flipped out the laws of Virginia. He turned to the page regarding those selected as electors and said, "Mr. Mitchell, I want to read you something. It is from the code of Virginia. The code states that you can ask a person who has come to register anything about his qualifications as an elector." Mr. Mitchell interrupted and said, "Elector?" "Yes, Mr. Mitchell. Elector. It is spelled E-l-e-c-t-o-r. That means he is potentially the person who can register to vote. Didn't you know that?" Mr. Adkins asked. Mr. Mitchell kind of hung his head and replied "Naw, I ain't never heard of 'dat." Mr. Adkins stated, "Mr. Mitchell, did you know this young man could take you to court for that?" Mr. Mitchell said, "Naw, I didn't know that! I'll put his name on 'da book!"

That's how Mert got registered to vote. He was the next person in the family after my father.

Well, I was so happy. I got my "A" in Mr. Adkins's class. Then I got my mother, two brothers, my oldest sister, and others in the community, even a man who couldn't write. He could write enough for him to understand it but no one else could. Mr. Mitchell had become so frightened by Mr. Adkins that I took nine persons at once and he passed everyone, including the man who couldn't write.

Even though I was too young to register myself, I felt energized by getting things done that white folks didn't want us to do. The whole process did serve to embolden me. I began to see the value in asserting myself against principles with which I disagreed.

That defiance in me surfaced years later when I went to teach in Emporia for my first teaching job. Now, I'm a civil rights person. I went to a NAACP meeting and I was the youngest there. There were only four persons present at the meeting: Samuel Tucker, who became a partner in the prominent law firm of Hill, Tucker and Marsh that had fought segregation; Rev. Dr. E. D. Shands, who had talked with me as a youngster about going to Virginia Seminary; Mr. Freeman, who owned a restaurant; and me. We talked about civil rights and I was feeling my oats.

Mr. Tucker said that there was a law that when you're traveling interstate by bus, you can sit wherever you want. Otherwise, by state law, blacks had to sit in the back. Mr. Tucker said he wanted some volunteers to travel from Emporia over to North Carolina, which would make us interstate passengers. The NAACP was asking if we would test that law to see if the states would try to enforce segregation on interstate passengers. Mr. Freeman and I volunteered.

When that day came, we also decided we were going to buy our tickets on the white side at the bus station. The plan was to board the bus, sit up front and take the ride. That was the test. We got in line and people were looking strangely at us, but we never said a word. When we got up to the counter, the cashier looked at us with surprise but said nothing and gave us our tickets. I thought he would not sell to us. We had our tickets, and went and sat down on the white side of the bus station. People just looked at us like we were aliens from another planet but nobody said a word. You could have heard a pin drop.

The announcement of our bus came over the loud speaker, and we got in line to board. Mr. Freeman was elderly, so he walked slowly, but we stayed together, gave the driver our tickets and sat in the front of the bus, right behind the driver. Mr. Freeman took the window seat and I took the aisle. We said nothing. When the driver finished collecting tickets and boarded the bus, he looked at us with astonishment. He also looked frightened but said not a word. Someone had told the bus drivers about the law, so he could not challenge us. The laws were slowly changing in our favor. We could have been mobbed or killed that day, but we were not. We made it back to where we started.

At the next NAACP meeting, we reported that between Emporia and Rocky Mount, North Carolina, they were not enforcing segregation. That doesn't sound like much now, but that was a big deal then because we could have been beaten or mobbed. This was a precursor to the famed bus rides of the era.

Civil rights and social justice have always been a part of my life, and these few stories have become a part of my spirit.

PART VI

Late Afternoon

Chapter Eleven

Eric's Birth, Gillfield's Special Supporters, and My Mother's Death

The Early Afternoon time frame of my life had ended. I watched these years roll by. As pastor, I continued to experience the joy of baptizing children, only to later marry them and then bless their babies. My family with Bertie continued to grow while my family in Brunswick County began to shrink. In 1969, Bertie and I had our fifth and final child.

We had thought that Herbert was going to be our last child, but then came Eric, and I was excited about his birth. It didn't really bother me whether this would be a boy or a girl because I already had two boys and two girls. I was thirty-seven years old when Eric was born on August 13, 1969. A good friend of mine named Dr. Bush delivered Eric, but there was a problem. Eric's health at birth was not good, and we had some real trying moments. Actually, Eric was ill before he was born. Bertie went to the hospital four times before he was born because there was the threat of losing the child. Dr. Bush helped to really guide us. When Eric was born, he was very weak and the doctor questioned whether he would live. I prayed so hard for him. For Dr. Samuel Bush's care and concern, I shall ever be grateful.

I remember the time when Eric was released from the hospital. There was joy and anxiety among us—joy because he was home, anxiety because his health issues remained on our minds. Eric, our baby, has brought us many happy moments as we added years. Today, he has a caring and concerned spirit—just like the family has had for him.

Gillfield was where most of my professional life's work took place, and I would like to take a moment to talk about some special persons in that church. I want to ask pardon for all the family members who will see only certain names in my autobiography because I cannot remember all of them. There were too many to recall. The pages would be filled with 200–300 people. But let me talk about a few of them who were very special.

I've already mentioned Deacon Burke. One of the things I thought was so interesting about Deacon Burke and his family was that each person in his family had three given names. He was named Henry Clifton Patrick Burke. He had a son, H. C. P. Burke, Jr., whom I didn't know and who died working in a laboratory at Tuskegee institute from some chemical that got loose in there. His elder daughter was named Mary Ellen Cecelia Burke. He had another son named James Wilbur Brown Burke, and a daughter named Thomasine Mason Lane Burke, the only child still living as this book is being written. She always breaks out into a great laugh when I see her because I'll say, "Hello, Thomasine Mason Lane Burke!" Deacon Burke was one of the special ones.

I want to mention Deacon William T. Greene, who was chairman of the deacon board. He was not a highly trained man but was head of building and grounds at Virginia State College. He was responsible for building two or three buildings at Virginia State with just common labor. He told me the story of how sometimes he didn't know what to do and would tell his men, "We'll work on that another day," and then go to something he knew. He was not an engineer. He said he would then go home and when he went to sleep at night, the Lord would give him what to do the next day. He never drove a car. He walked from his home on Wilcox Street to Virginia State College and was on the job every morning at 7:30 A.M. He was such a well-wisher and such an easy man to get along with, and I needed that because I was so young when I came to Gillfield. He respected me as his pastor. He wouldn't do a thing without sitting down and talking to me. Deacon Greene was very special.

Another special person was Richard W. Pegram. We called him Dick Pegram and he called me Pal. He called most men Pal. He was an educator who worked at Peabody High School. He was not one who was in the high academic circles, but he was an administrative assistant. He would see to it that the students got their books. He would stand in the hallway to see that the students got to their classes. He had a wonderful relationship with the students. He just got along with everybody, as did Deacon Greene. Those are the type of people you need around you in order to be successful. He was so supportive of me. He would tell me things like "Pal, I think you ought not do that" or "Pal, this would be a good thing to do." He lived a half block from me and would even come by my house sometimes just to play checkers.

Another person I recall was Sadie E. Roberts, who also lived within walking distance from my house, just across the street from Dick Pegram. She never married. Miss Roberts was on the board of finance at Gillfield. She wore the finest clothes and had the finest furniture. In fact, when she left Petersburg at the age of ninety-four, her niece from New Jersey gave me a hat stand that I have today in my den. That stand actually belonged to her mother and is about two hundred years old. She gave the church a couch that is in the narthex right now.

Truthfully, I can say now that Miss Roberts was a gossiper. She loved to talk about things that I didn't know. She would tell me about people who had problems fifty years ago. She would say, "You know, everybody didn't die at the same time."

Ms. Roberts helped me when we were going to build the Christian Education Center. I had a serious problem with some members, one in particular, who was holding me up with some legal things. I was worried. I went to Ms. Roberts's house around the corner and I said to her rather quietly, "Ms. Roberts, I don't think I can be pastor of this church much longer." She said, "Why?" I told her the problem but said I couldn't mention names and I left her house. That was in the morning. Later that afternoon, Ms. Roberts came to my house with four other women. They said if anyone would stand in my way to build the Christian Education Center, just let them know and they would make a motion to take them off any board or committee where they stood in the way. The person got the message and stopped his opposition.

During this period, heavy finances were needed for the acquisition of land and for the down payment on a loan from the bank. (The bank had said we needed to raise $20,000 in six weeks, over and above our normal income.) Russell L. Bland, chair of the finance committee, played a most significant role in meeting this and related responsibilities.

Another significant person in Gillfield was Nathaniel Gatlin. He was a deacon when I first got to Gillfield. He told me within the first two weeks of my pastorate that when his term was up, he would not take another term. He stated that the reason for his withdrawal was not because of me and he wanted me to know it in advance. The reason was that when he became a deacon, he told Wyatt Walker that he would serve one term because he was so busy as chairman of the music department at Virginia State. They were getting ready to do some things that he needed to focus on, such as a foreign trip.

I talked confidentially with Dr. Gatlin about my interest in getting a choir director. He said that Virginia State was hiring a man from Louisiana who was a director with a master's degree. His name was Willis C. Patterson, and Dr. Gatlin was bringing him in because he wanted to expand his music department to include someone with voice training. When Mr. Patterson came to Virginia State, he started the opera workshop. Patterson was the black person who sang on NBC in the opera called *Amahl and the Night Visitors*, by Menotti. Patterson not only had talent but he brought culture and image to the school.

He came to Gillfield as choir director and raised the choir singing to a more excellent level. He was the one who really brought hymn singing and anthems to Gillfield. When he left Gillfield, he became head of the music department at the University of Michigan.

Dr. Gatlin was instrumental in helping me to pull in music people, both students and professors. At that time, I needed an organist, because Mrs. Williams was scaling back. Dr. Gatlin said, "Reverend, don't get anyone right now. I'm bringing in someone in September that you will love. He has his degree in choral conducting and he's a great organist and pianist. I'm going to talk with him." His name was Dr. Carl Gordon Harris and I was able to hire him. I would have had him direct the choir, but a member of the church had been recommended by Mrs. Williams and I couldn't upset the family relationships. Dr. Harris was the finest musician and influenced music in the church. He was so gifted as a pianist and organist and he had his doctorate in choral conducting. Carl started for me the Heritage Chorale, which brought some wonderful Negro spirituals into the church. These two outstanding musicians, Dr. Harris and Mr. Patterson, lifted the level of music at Gillfield tremendously and both came via one Nathaniel F. Gatlin.

Ruby James was superintendant of Sunday school when I came to Gillfield. She was principal of Westview Elementary, which was a new school in Petersburg at the time. She brought the educational image, and the teachers of our Sunday school respected her. So I was able to work with her to merge a Sunday school and Christian education program at the same time. Ruby James was a wonderful person.

Louise Jackson Thompson was truly an educator. She looked like an educator. She walked like an educator and she talked like an educator. She would say, "Yes! No! . . . Of course!" She was such a friend. I named her Administrative Assistant (volunteer). It is too much for me to enumerate the many quality projects she implemented.

Thomas Rudolph Reid. We called him "Speedy Reid." I called him a man for all seasons. He was truly a gifted person for anything needed. He would even prepare artistic bulletins for me. He wasn't a typist but he would write them out. He recited poetry. He was involved in our Sunday school program and he influenced people. He was very outspoken in a kind of hilarious way that you would have to laugh at rather than be offended.

His greatest gift was in food service, and he was head of food service at Virginia State. Someone once said there were three bosses at Virginia State: R. P. Daniel, the president; Charlie Towne, the physician; and Thomas Reid, who really ran the school. He would tell the president what was to be done. Every Friday after Thanksgiving, he had my family over to his home, and he would serve us a nine-course meal. He had built a back room where he had the most beautiful dining room table that sat about twenty-four people. He had the most beautiful tablecloths you had ever seen.

Mr. Reid was the greatest entertainer and would often end our meals at his house by reading poetry or serving ice cream that would be on fire, which my children thought was wonderful! He played the piano and walked so fast. That's why we called him Speedy Reid. He entertained people like Martin L. King, Jr., Mordecai Johnson, Benjamin Mays, and others. Whoever was a guest of the president of Virginia State was a guest of Thomas Reid and he had pictures with all these people. Thomas Reid was a great influence. I asked him once how he made a cucumber soup he had prepared. I don't know what he put in it, but it was really delicious! I said, "Mr. Reid, I know you don't like to tell how you fix things, but would you tell me how you make cucumber soup? I'd like to make some." He said, "Well, let me tell you, Reverend, what you do. First, you go out and buy yourself some cucumbers. Then, you come back to me and I might want to talk to you!" He wouldn't tell me!

There's one more incident I'd like to share involving Speedy Reid. It was so funny. My son Grady Jr. graduated from Howard University. He had fallen in love with a young lady on the campus named Danette Denson and he wanted to marry her. They wanted to marry in the chapel of Howard University's Law School. There were people from Petersburg, of course, who wanted to attend, and they decided to have a bus load of people from Gillfield travel to Washington. Reid was on the bus with all the other members.

What a big day it was! I was going to perform my son's wedding in the law school chapel. Herbert Conway and Eric Charles were in the ceremony. It was a hot day and the wedding went on as planned and then we had the reception. I don't know who was responsible for the reception, but they were moving awfully slow and I'm sure the heels under Speedy Reid's feet were on fire. So, without any consent from me or anyone there, Reid jumped into action, and the next thing I knew, Thomas Reid was behind the table and he just took over! It was as if he were throwing plates over his head. I've laughed about that to this day, but Thomas Reid saw to it that the reception proceeded as it should. We have a picture of Thomas Reid assisting Grady Jr. and Danette as they cut the cake!

These are just a few of the people with whom I interacted on a close basis at Gillfield and surely, there were many, many others. Good memories, good people, and good times . . . and time continued to move on.

Surely as the sun does shine and the good times roll, there will also be dark days and storms in our lives that are unavoidable. It's a part of living.

I lost my mother in 1965. I think one of the greatest problems I saw family-wise was to witness the deterioration of my mother. She had always been a full-bodied woman and she started to lose weight. She started to lose the dexterity of her hands, and since she had always done the cooking, this had a major impact on the household. Daddy couldn't cook. Then we noticed that she started losing her mind, so she went to stay with my sister Mable. Doctors confirmed the deterioration of her mind. She stayed with Mable a while and then she came to stay with me. I saw her confusion, and it broke my heart.

She was in our guest room and would call out to me, "Grady! Grady! The bees are coming to sting me! You see all those bees!" I said, "Mama, there are no bees up there." She would reply, "Can't you see those bees!" I would go to the wall where she said she saw bees and try to show her there were no bees there by rubbing my hand against the wall. She would still insist there were bees and would yell out to me, "Don't do that Grady! Those bees are going to sting you!"

We still thought that Mom was physically going to live for a long time. I put her in the hospital while I took my family to Pittsburgh for our annual vacation. It was the summer of 1965 and we were just going to stay two weeks this time. Normally we stayed for a month. I went out to play golf with Bertie's aunt's husband in Vandergrift, Pennsylvania, and when I got back that evening, I was told my mother had died.

We had to pack up and come right back. It was shocking because if I had ever thought that I was going to lose my mother, I would not have gone. That's the story of my mother's death, which was quite an adjustment. It was only the second time I had lost a close relative. The time before was in 1947, when my oldest brother was killed. I was only fifteen years old when Buster died. Each death was like a violent storm. Somehow I survived each one and was able to carry on amongst the living.

CHAPTER TWELVE

Surviving the Storms

The grass is cut by a lawn mower only to grow back again. Homes and cars are purchased only to later be sold or consumed by damage. They are replaced or rebuilt. People, however, cannot be replaced. When they exit life's stage, they are not coming back. That which is left to us is their memory and the times we shared together.

I remember losing my brother Buster. It was very traumatic for me at fifteen years old. I was the youngest child and Buster was the oldest. I always looked up to Buster. He was kind of my idol. He joined the Navy when few people from our area did this. I didn't know anyone who had been to the Navy except Buster. I had two brothers who joined the Army, but Buster went to the Navy. My two brothers who went to the Army had Army uniforms. Buster had a blue suit and it looked so nice and official. He had a white cap. He just looked good in his uniform.

Buster was courting Mariah Kelly and they were going to be married. There was not to be a big celebration at a church. The family was not going to attend his wedding as we do today. He was simply going to marry her at her house. We didn't have weddings out in the country. People just got married and would come back and say "We're married!" We would respond, "Is that right? Well, congratulations!"

The night before Buster was to marry Mariah, Buster and several of his friends went out for a meeting of The Ante Red Sox. After the game, they went to Emporia to the movies. When they returned, they stopped by Jody Williams's store. Much later, I was told that a white man came to the store to challenge a black man because the black man was courting a black girl who was the white man's girlfriend. The white man said, "Didn't I tell you to leave my woman alone!" He pulled out a gun and shot at the black man, who ducked. The bullet hit Buster in the temple and he was dead. Buster was dragged from the store and put up at the corner. The white man dared anyone to tell what had happened. He said, "If anybody says what happened here, I'm going to get you!"

In the midst of the night, we heard someone yelling out to my mother, "Lilly, Lilly, Lilly! Open the door!" She came to the door and said, "Who's there?" The gentleman replied, "I'm Junior Mitchell! Buster is dead down the road!" My mother started screaming and I awoke amid all the commotion. Buster was dead and we all were in shock. It was as if a tornado had come through the house. They took Daddy down there and Mama just started running from the house. Percy and I followed her. We caught her at the road and she was crying. We were in our shorts. We just had to catch her. She had almost gone berserk. Daddy got back home and confirmed that Buster was dead. He was the first sibling I'd lost and he was murdered.

After my mother's death, we all regrouped around Daddy. We would go to Toot's home and Daddy would be there. The memory of Mama was all around. Daddy loved his grandchildren and there is a treasured family picture with Daddy and all his grandchildren surrounding him at Toot's house. Grady Jr. is sitting on Daddy's knee as a little boy. We rallied around him and became very protective and supportive of him.

I suggested to Daddy that he come to Petersburg and stay with Bertie and me through the winter. So he came in November. I remember so clearly his arrival in Petersburg. It was the second Sunday in November 1965. He came that afternoon by bus and I met him at the station. At that time, we were having communion at night at Gillfield, and Daddy went with me. The ladies of the church knew that Mama had died, and they were trying to make him feel better. So they were all coming to greet and speak to him. There were seven widows at the church that night and they were all attempting to "get Mr. Powell." Daddy was so proud. When they finished with him, and I knew they were joking with him, I said, "Come on, Daddy, let's go to my office."

It was then that I heard the voice of someone who would intercept the final years of my Daddy's life. The voice said, "Rev. Powell, you haven't introduced me to your father."

I said, "Daddy, come here. This is Miss Annie Mae Evans. We call her Miss Annie Mae." She liked that introduction and she took Daddy's old, rough, country hand and said, "You have such a fine son," and she patted his hand several times. "You have such a fine son," she repeated. "He works so hard," she added. I noticed how Daddy seemed to enjoy her attention. We finished talking to her and I went upstairs, took my robe off, and we went home. I didn't think much of that encounter with Annie Mae, but Lord if I only knew what was going to happen, I would have thrown him over my shoulders and rushed him into my office when I heard her voice.

The following morning I said, "Daddy, I want you to go with me to church." I thought my children would worry him because they always wanted to sit on his lap. He would play a game with my kids called "Hickedy-Hackedy-Horndid-cup. How many fingers do I hold up? Two you said and two it was. Now young man your time is up!" So Daddy agreed to go with me to church. He always loved to read the paper in the morning, so I picked up the morning paper and a few magazines. About 11:00 A.M. I said, "Daddy, I'm going to take you by some of these widows' homes." I wanted him to be happy, you know. Mamma was gone.

So I took him by Mrs. Crowder's and to visit Miss Mattie Perry, whose late husband was the treasurer of the church when I came. She laughed a lot with him and he had a nice time with both women. I then took him to visit Mrs. Holmes, who was a member of First Baptist Church. She had a very distinguishable laugh and we all laughed together. Her husband had built the parsonage in which I lived. He was from Brunswick County, I might add. Then I took him by Miss Annie Mae's. She was kind of serious. She said to me, "Rev. Powell, you work so hard. Why don't you leave your Daddy here and I'll fix him lunch. When you go to pick up your wife later this afternoon, you can pick him up then." In other words, "Why don't you get lost while I spin my web around this man!" But truly at the time, I didn't think much of it and really thought to myself, "Isn't that nice of her to do this so I can get some work done."

I came back to pick up Daddy later as planned and I wanted to pick the old boy's brain and just kind of see what went on at Annie Mae's. All I could get out of Daddy was "She's nice company."

"Daddy what did you all talk about?" I prodded.

"She's nice company," he repeated. So that was that and he decided to stay at my home the rest of the day.

Daddy continued to stay with us for brief periods. On one occasion, I wanted him to come back to be with Bertie while I was out of town preaching at Saint Paul's College. Bertie doesn't like to be home alone. The details of his departure and return were set and I wasn't expecting him to be there when I returned, but he was. I thought maybe he was enjoying the children. Bertie said, "Grady come here with me to the kitchen for a moment. I've got something to tell you. Your Daddy's going to get married!" "What!" I replied in horror. "He's going to get married to whom?" "Miss Annie Mae," Bertie answered. I said, "He just met her three weeks ago!" Well, here we go.

I said begrudgingly, "Daddy, come in here." He came in smiling sheepishly and I said, "Daddy, I understand from Bertie that you are planning to marry Miss Annie Mae."

"Yes, I am," he firmly replied.

"Well congratulations, Daddy. I want the best for you and if this is what you want, then that's fine. You know you sent me to college and were supportive of me when I gave up teaching and went into seminary. One of my courses was in counseling and one of my responsibilities was to counsel people before they get married. I'd just like us to sit down and talk about this."

He said, "Listen, Grady," and crooked his finger at me, the way he did whenever he gestured to make a point. "Your counseling is for your members," he continued, "but I'm your Daddy and you can't tell me nothing." Bertie broke out in a cry. She wanted him to wait at least a year since Mama had just passed away four months before.

The fact is that my father was adamant about getting married. I really believe, however, that he wasn't as adamant about getting married as the lady who was about to marry him was. For some reason I think in her spirit she thought marrying the pastor's daddy would make her more appealing to Gillfield members. She had really outsmarted my daddy, and he became determined to get married. My siblings were highly opposed to it and so was I. I changed my opinion, however, and the reason was that my father came to me and I saw that he was sad. He said, "Grady, I want you to talk to your sister Mable." I said, "Talk to her about what?" He replied with a tinge of sadness, "Read this letter." I read it and in it she said every ugly thing that she possibly could. She was angry about his getting married. I was hurt after reading the letter and I suddenly felt sorry for him. I immediately changed my position and said to him, "Daddy, I'll talk to Mable and I'll perform your wedding." They were married in the parsonage and that was that.

My daddy's second marriage wasn't all that he had anticipated. There was a nagging question about whether Miss Annie Mae had been married to a man named Mr. Evans, as she said she had been, or if the two of them had merely been shacking up. I asked Daddy to ask Miss Annie Mae to show him those marriage papers, but in the end, they were never produced, even though he asked her. Before his life ended, Daddy realized she had fooled him about being married to Mr. Evans for all those years she lived with him, and he was sad about being manipulated.

The only thing I can say that was good about his marriage to Miss Annie Mae is that it allowed him to return to his home, which is where he wanted to be, and she cooked for him. He got serious stomach cancer in the end, and she stayed with him while he suffered. In 1972, Daddy died. It had been only three years since Mamma died and now he was gone. We were all heartbroken. Mable was torn apart, and I remember her just screaming when she heard the news. We had to regroup again just as we had done when Mama died.

Percy, Mert, Toot, Irene, Mable, and I remained. The third Sunday in August we would get together at Toot's house just like we did with Daddy after Mama died. Mable would arrive on Friday and start the cooking. She was full-bodied, and always put her apron on. Mable was a great cook. I would bring maybe three watermelons and sodas. We would have the time of our lives, the six of us.

In 1981, Percy died. He died one month after Sandra and Dot had married. The last time I saw Percy was at church at the wedding. I had on my formal clothes. Percy wanted to say something crazy and he said, "Grady, where's the toilet?" I said, "In your pants!" We laughed together. My siblings left the church and returned to Brunswick County. That was the last thing we said to each other. Thirty days later I was sitting on the couch and I heard Bertie scream. It was June of 1981. I said, "What's wrong?" She said, "Percy is dead!" "What!" I responded. I grabbed the phone and said, "What's happened?" Percy was only in his fifties. They were outside cooking steaks and when Percy leaned down to light the fire, they said he just hollered out, "Oh boy!" and down on the ground he went. He was dead. Heart attack. Vivian, my niece, said Mert started trembling; he was so upset. Another storm had come.

Then, about two years after Percy died, I got a call about 1:30 A.M. in the morning from Ophelia. "Uncle Grady, we've taken Daddy to the hospital!" She was speaking of Mert. I said, "What's wrong?" She replied, "Daddy's just spitting up and I tell you, Uncle Grady, I don't think Daddy's going to make it!" The next call I got, he was dead. He was really dead, Ophelia said, when they left home. He'd had a heart attack.

Then there came Mable. Bertie said Mable had become my second mother. After my two brothers passed, the children who remained re-grouped. I have many pictures that show how we became closer as our family started to thin out. There's a picture of Irene and me dancing. We regrouped, but then Mable died.

Mable was kind of the glue that held us together after our parents passed. She was the oldest, and I would go to Mable's every Tuesday be-cause of her illness. We would go to her doctor's appointment together and come back home and eat. Mable would cook just what I wanted: pig feet, chitlins, collard greens, corn bread—all the stuff I loved.

Well, one day I took Mable to the doctor and she mentioned to me before we arrived that she wanted to tell the doctor her navel felt warm. The doctor told her that her navel was never tied correctly and therefore was subject to getting bacteria in it. The doctor said it could be corrected. Before any type of surgery, a blood test is required. So I took Mable for her blood test. There were some X-rays made and that's when lung cancer was discovered. Mable had never smoked one cigarette in her whole life. The doctor suggested that the cancerous lung be removed and Mable agreed. In spite of it, Mable and I joked around. I found a quiet place in the hospital to pray for her and I returned home. I thought about how she was always there for me, from taking me to get my shots for school to watching over me as I worked in the farm fields, and just there for me when sometimes I needed to talk to a family member.

Surgery was scheduled, and it was successful. In the meantime, my sons were arriving from California for my anniversary celebration at Gillfield. When I got home from picking up one of them from the airport, Bertie met me at the door and said, "Grady! Mable is sick unto death!" "What?" I replied. She was doing so well when I went to see her. She had already had the surgery. Yet, when I got to the hospital, Mable was unconscious, and in a couple of hours, she was dead. Mable was gone. Shocking. It was as if one of my appendages had fallen off. My anniversary celebration now had a major storm cloud hanging over it. With my children arriving at the house, I did my best to contain myself but I could not.

I left the house and went into the backyard and just worked on the flowerpots hanging from the trees, watering them and pulling dead leaves. The water from the water jug might as well have been connected to my eyes, for the tears would not stop. Grady Jr. followed me into the backyard. He knew his daddy was heartbroken. He ended up in the driveway leaning over one of the cars as he cried. He told me later he had never seen his dad cry. "Surviving the storms" is passed down from generation to generation. We cry together, and then we regroup and find the strength to carry on.

Now with Mable gone, that left Toot, Irene, and me. What do we do? We regrouped. We worked hard to pull together Mable's affairs after she passed. I was her administrator and worked for three years to complete her administrative details. In the meantime, while I was working as Mable's administrator, Irene came to me after one of my vacations and said, "Grady, I didn't want to tell you this until you got back from vacation, but I need to have another operation. The pig's valve that was put in me six to eight years ago is coming loose. The doctor said if I sneeze too hard, it might shake it loose and death would be instant." It was attached to her heart. Oh my God, was that something to hear. Irene had to go back for heart surgery. Wow!

While this was going on, Toot had a heart attack and went to McGuire Hospital. While Toot was at McGuire Hospital, Irene had to go to the hospital for her heart surgery. She didn't make it. I had to go and tell Toot that Irene had died while he was lying in a hospital bed from a heart attack. We were both overcome with grief.

Now it was down to just Toot and me. You know what we did? We regrouped. I would find any reason I could to call Toot, and it was usually about the garden. We grew up together working Daddy's tobacco and cornfields. After I left Brunswick County, Toot remained there and over the years had become a gardening expert. I mean, he really knew gardening, so I would call him. We would go on and on about one thing to the next. Toot would come by house here in Camelot and we would go to my garden. He would look around and say, "Grady you ain't got nothin' here. Why you have this little garden, Grady?" I would just laugh, and we would laugh together.

Well, Toot and I were able to share many years together and many good times after everyone else in the family had checked out. But before I knew it, Toot was gone. He died within hours of his wife's passing. Ruth had meant so much to him, I just think when she left, he wanted to go with her. There was a joint funeral for them.

When Toot died, I really felt alone. Everybody in my family had died but me. I think Toot's death probably was the hardest. I felt so alone. The suddenness of it. I had just seen him that afternoon, and within two hours, he was dead. That was the hardest. As I sit here and talk about this, I become emotional to tears because it's not easy. It really isn't.

I think my children and my wife have helped me to survive these tremendous storms of life. Oh yes. Really, really rough. Nobody left but me. Bertie has helped me tremendously get through these tough times. A wife, however, is not like a sibling. You see, with a sibling you've had to survive so many conflicts together. The children in your life are altogether different. They represent a different kind of support group. They bring their love, a type of love a spouse can't give, and a spouse brings a type of love that children can't give.

I remember an occurrence that was so very meaningful to me when Toot passed. I'll never forget it. On the night he died I was sitting at home when someone knocked on the playroom door. "Who is it?" I ask. "Daddy, it's Sandra and Albert." I open the door and she just hugged me and said, "I've come to be with my daddy!" That was so meaningful to me.

I have learned something over these years about surviving the storms, and it's a song:

> For I know whate'er befalls me,
> Jesus doeth all things well.

That's what I have learned. That song means to me that it doesn't matter how bad it is, just stay alive and something good will come out of it.

Also, my interpretation of the Old Testament story of Joseph in Egypt coincides with this belief. Isaac, Joseph's father, favored Joseph over his other twelve sons and gave him a "coat of many colors." Joseph's journey through life led him from being a selfish brat, through sibling anger and cruelty, to a place of power and prominence. Because of past problems, his brothers feared that he would kill them since he had so much power over them. They knew they had thrown him down a well to die when he was a brat and the favorite son of their father. Joseph said in conclusion that what they had done to him as a youngster, they had meant for evil, but God had used it for good.

The story of Joseph and his brothers is one that documents the pain and suffering that Joseph endured but shows that God can take a situation that seems hopeless and turn it into good. My theme still is "I know whate'er befalls me, Jesus doeth all things well." So in the storms of my life, I have had to find ways to turn the trials into something good, and through the goodness and mercy of God, I've survived these deadly storms.

I've had storms in the church. I've had storms in my personal life. I've had storms in rearing my children. I've had storms in school. But I've leaned back on that theme and said, "For I know whate'er befalls me, Jesus doeth all things well." That's my theme and I'll go to my grave with that thought in my heart.

PART VII

Evening

Chapter Thirteen

Friends, Women Deacons, and Reflections

I worked hard at Gillfield. Let nobody fool you. I believe that a pastor ought to get up in the morning, have breakfast with his family, and go out to work, and I did this every day. I would cook breakfast for the family while Bertie would get the children corralled and dressed for school. Generally, I was at Gillfield about 7:30 in the morning.

What do you do when you sit down in an office as pastor? One of the first things I did when I came to Gillfield was clip out any piece of paper about any church member and make a file on every single one. Actually, I kept a file on every member for thirty-five years. It's still at the church to this day.

Again and again I would ask myself, "What do you do?" You train children before you baptize them. You go to the hospital and see people who are sick. When do you do it? You can do it early in the morning, or any other time of the day! What do you do as a pastor? You get involved in the local community, membership affairs, state-level ecclesiastical interests (e.g. Baptist General Conventions), and national and international activities (e.g. American Baptist Churches, USA).

One of my goals as pastor of Gillfield was to be involved with ecclesiastical matters pertaining to the church as an organization. For example, when I came to Gillfield, I read in the paper that there was to be a meeting of the Petersburg Ministerial Union. This was not an integrated group; it was all white. I had been a member of the Richmond Clergy Association when I was at Quioccasin, so I wanted to be a part of this in Petersburg. The month was September. The paper said the meeting of the Petersburg Ministerial Union was on Monday at the corner of

Washington and Dunlop streets. I couldn't find any of my close associates who were members: Gilmore wasn't a member; Wyatt wasn't a member; Reid wasn't a member; nor was L. C. Johnson. I went in, however, as if I thought it was integrated.

I walked in and said, "I'm Grady Powell. I'm the pastor of Gillfield Baptist Church." "How are you, Grady?" they responded. There were no blacks there. I met three people who welcomed me so much. Bob Vaughn was one. He was the pastor of Second Presbyterian Church. Boston Lackey was another. He was priest of Christ and Grace Episcopal Church. I met Solomon Jacobson, who was the rabbi of Temple Brith Achim. Boston Lackey said later that they didn't know what to do with me, but as time progressed, we all worked things out and became close colleagues. Surprisingly enough, at my installation, Solomon Jacobson was a program participant. He was president of the Petersburg Ministerial Union. I approached my time at Gillfield with a sense of ecclesiastical community expansion. In other words, there was work to do in the church, but Gillfield was also a part of a community and I had to reach out in that community as a representative of Gillfield and its members.

I got to know a man named Linwood E. Horne, who was pastor of Walnut Hill Baptist Church, a predominantly white church. He and I became good friends. He left Walnut Hill and became religious leader at the University of Richmond. I knew Dr. Horne at UR! He was a fine man! He invited me to become a member of the book club at the university. Succeeding him at Walnut Hill Baptist Church was a man named Glenn Plot, who became one of my best friends. He helped in terms of the ecumenical movement and in terms of the interracial movement. His children became friends with my children. He taught his children and congregation that people are more than the color of their skin.

I have had a lot of preacher friends who have been supportive of me, as well as friends who are not clergy. It's been beyond denomination. It has been beyond race. Robert Gilmore Williams, who was at Zion Baptist Church when I came to Petersburg, became a wonderful friend. He was my laughing buddy. He was funny—beyond funny. Then there were those whom I went to school with who joined the church where I was pastor: Lawrence Pollard and Harold Braxton. They both were working in Petersburg and are lifelong friends to this day. Harold is another buddy who can tell joke after joke and keep on going with another joke. I remember Harold would come over to the parsonage when we would have parties and holler scary things up the stairs to the children and then just start laughing. Harold and Pollard both are just great guys and truly dear friends.

Then there is my friend Jack White, known to the Petersburg community as Rev. Andrew J. White. He succeeded Bob Gilmore at Zion Baptist Church. Jack and I have been colleagues over a long period of time, and our congregations have been partners in several ministries. His son Andy and my son Grady Jr. became close friends when they were in school together in Petersburg. Grady Jr. would go to Jack's house on Adams Street with Andy after school every day until we would come and pick him up. Although they live in different areas of Virginia today, they remain friends.

I also want to mention Ed Coleman, who was unusual in his friendship. When we were talking about the needs of Petersburg early in my pastorate, he found out what I wanted to do and helped me raise over $3,000 in order to start a child care center that was to be located right near the church. Ed Coleman was meaningful to me. I've had many supportive people to help me in the development of Gillfield, including Teresa Green, Helen Crowder, and Gertrude Clark, who were so very kind to our family from day one. Elsie and Cordlandt Colson, Walker H. Quarles, and later on, Huey Battle and his wife Jimmy are on a long list of persons who helped me in the work of the church. In addition, Doris W. Adkins has been a significant leader and constant friend throughout my pastorate. With excellence, she served as treasurer for many years (following the death of her husband, whom she succeeded as treasurer). She brought to this responsibility real dedicated service and the best in bookkeeping and related services. There were many other people at Gillfield who were helpful, but if I named them all, that would consume the rest of this book. However, I'm so grateful to all my friends and colleagues who made my work and my life meaningful and effective.

As I consider the people who supported the ministry of the church, I recall the women who were spiritual leaders, and recall when we decided to have women deacons at Gillfield Baptist Church.

Gillfield was the first African American Baptist church in the United States to have women deacons. That decision came through the American Baptist Convention indirectly. I was a member of the board of education and we met quarterly in various parts of the country. Dr. Harold Richardson announced his retirement as Executive Minister for the Board of Education of American Baptist. The search committee went about its work and there was to be a related meeting in Harrisburg, Pennsylvania. The search committee wrote us and said they were going to be recommending a Rev. Robert Campbell from California. A résumé was distributed about him and it demonstrated the quality of man he was. He had been quite a leader with American Baptist.

Subsequently, I received a telegram from the women of the board of education in the National Convention. One of them I remember. Her name was Lois Blankenship. The telegram stated that they thought Rev. Campbell was a wonderful candidate, but they were disappointed in the search committee. They went on to state that the search committee had invited only men to apply. Not one woman was invited to apply and I thought it was terrible. It was similar to what had happened to blacks. There I was, the only black person from the South, and I decided I had to speak up against this, I had to. I knew what had happened to us as black people, so I understood the pain of being discriminated against.

I flew up to Harrisburg, and when the report of the search committee was given, I stood on the floor to speak. I told them about what I had experienced in Petersburg and the South with discrimination. I told them I was certain that very few people really disliked me because I was black. In fact, they didn't dislike Negroes. They just never bothered to ask blacks if they wanted to have this position or that job—they just never asked. I felt the audience understood the connection. When I finished my statement and the meeting was over, those women in that department took to me like glue with gratitude for my statement. I felt good about having the courage to speak up for those left out of society.

It was time to fly back home. The plane was in the air, and before we could even reach our traveling height, I began to figuratively pat myself on the back and say to myself, "Grady, you really did what you should have done. The American Baptist needed to hear that." As quickly as those laudatory comments were coming into my brain, there was another thought that said, "You've done the same to women at Gillfield as the American Baptist did to their women members. You have a board of deacons in the church you serve and no one has ever invited a woman to serve on that board in the church's 170-year history." I became ashamed of myself. I started praying, "Lord, if you just let me get on the ground from this plane, I'm going to work on a plan to invite women to join the board of deacons."

At the first deacons meeting, I told the deacons about my experience at American Baptist and said that I thought we should consider women deacons. You know what they did? They laughed at me. That laugh meant, "Reverend, you've got to be kidding! Do you know what you're talking about?" I backed off because I could see that there was no need to push this battle right then. It wasn't going to work. You have to learn when to fight battles. This was a battle, however, that I was not going to give up. It was just a matter of timing and when I was going to reengage the participants.

I decided that I was going to study this thing, and I got every book I could find about women in the church. There was one book by O. John Eldred. The book was entitled *Women Pastors: If God Calls, Why Not the Church?* Eldred was director of education for American Baptist of the South and gave up his job to follow his wife on a professional decision, which required moving to another state. Men don't usually do that. It's normally the other way around.

As pastor of the church, I was able to start off any board or group meeting with a fifteen-minute statement on any subject I wanted. So over the next year, I had all the different boards and committees at Gillfield studying the subject of the possibility of women as deacons. I read from books like John Eldred's and I would quote scripture on the subject.

As we began to approach the next annual meeting, I started approaching certain women at Gillfield and simply asking, "Would you be willing to serve as a deacon?" I went to Doris Adkins, a dedicated member and a very intelligent person. She said, "Oh no! I couldn't have my husband saying 'my wife is a deacon.' It would embarrass him!" It was a foreign idea to men and women. I approached Agnes Morgan. She started laughing and said, "Oh Lord no, Reverend!" She laughed with good intention. New ideas are hard to wrap yourself around.

I went to Lula Allgood, another woman, who like Doris and Agnes was fully dedicated to the work of the church. She was highly educated and the principal of a school. I sat down and talked with her and she said, "Lord, Reverend . . . Lord, Reverend! I guess my daddy, who was a deacon, would think it's crazy that I would think about it. But you think I could be a deacon?" I said, "I think so, Lula." She responded, "If the church wants me, I'd be willing to serve." That was the first one.

Now with Lula's willingness to try, I wanted to pick someone else who wasn't as high up in the education field. If you're going to start a precedent, start it right. Show that all people from all walks of life are invited to serve. Some people had already said, "You have to have a college degree to be a member of Gillfield," so I wanted to pop that bubble in this precedent.

I decided to go to a lady that I had found to be very dedicated, particularly in the program of music. She was also a business owner. She was a beautician and she dressed like the Queen of England, always sharp and ready for any occasion with the right outfit. Her name: Barbara Myles. I approached her and she said, "What!" I said, "Would you, Barbara?" She replied with glee, "Yes! Yes, Reverend! I'll do it!"

Then I had to get the nominating committee together. We took it to the church's annual meeting and everybody voted for it but two. The two who voted against it were Charles Wiggins, chairman of the deacon board, and his wife. Majority rules, however, and Lula and Barbara were installed as the first African American Baptist women to serve as deacons in the United States. ABC News sent a camera crew to Gillfield for an interview, and the rest is history.

Maybe ten years later, I stopped by to see the Wiggins one morning because they wanted to see me about a car. Mrs. Wiggins said, "Rev. Powell, I just want to say something to you. You remember when we voted against having women deacons?" I said, "Yes, I remember." She continued, "I'm so glad we were outvoted! Barbara Myles is our deacon now and you can't get a better deacon in this world."

One of the biggest physical accomplishments I had at Gillfield was the completed construction of the Christian Education Center. The reason it was the biggest was because we had no African American church in Petersburg that had ever built a Christian Education Center. So the idea was new. We still have a picture of the ground-breaking ceremony lying around Gillfield somewhere. I think it's in the Heritage Room. Mr. William Baugh, a trustee, was in the picture wearing an overcoat. It was kind of cool outside that day.

There were two things working against us. The first one was that when I started mentioning this idea to members, people said Brown & Williamson Tobacco Company was preparing to take the church property by eminent domain laws and therefore we should move to Ettrick and build a new church. Many people from the Virginia State community supported that idea. The second difficulty was that we had no space to build.

So how could I tackle the first objection? One way was to simply go directly to Brown & Williamson and have a discussion. I went to them and met with a man named Mr. McDonald and asked him about the rumor I'd heard about Brown & Williamson taking over our property. Brown & Williamson was so important to the city of Petersburg that if they had gone to the city council and said they wanted that space, I believe the city council would have voted in their favor for eminent domain and there would have been nothing we could do. Eminent domain has been a national law since the founding of this country and a judge simply says, "Give them a fair price."

So I sat down next with the chief executive and he said, "You know, I haven't heard of anybody saying that here at Brown & Williamson, but in two weeks I'm going to Louisville for a meeting and I'll discuss it further while I'm there." When he returned from the meeting he called me and I went to see him. He said that upper management replied that they had no thought of taking our building. They further stated that we were there before they were and they wanted to be good neighbors. He concluded by saying that if there was anything that Brown & Williamson could do for Gillfield Baptist Church, they would do it.

In spite of this neighborly decision by Brown & Williamson, the rumors continued. Rumors are terrible. They spread like a fire in a forest. One rumor stated that we ran Brown & Williamson out of town because we wouldn't sell them our building. Many years later, after Brown & Williamson was long gone, I was down at the tax place and heard one man say to another, "Isn't it a shame. I used to work at B & W and I was making twice as much as I'm making now." The other man replied, "You know why B & W isn't here anymore, don't you?" The man responded, "No, I don't." The gentleman concluded, "That church did it. What's the name of that church? I forgot, but B & W offered that church three million dollars and they wouldn't take it, so the company left and went somewhere else." I like to tell that story because you wonder sometimes, how do rumors start and gather misinformation as they keep rolling?

So I came back to the members of Gillfield, now knowing that Brown & Williamson wanted to help us. I also felt that some people in our church wanted us to move to Ettrick irrespective of Brown & Williamson. I wanted Gillfield to stay in the downtown Petersburg area where we were. I thought it was such a historic area. I went to some women in the church to discuss the matter. One of those women was Jessie Stith Green. I asked her, "Ms. Green, how do you feel about us moving to Ettrick?" Her quick response was, "Moving? What are you talking about?" I led her to believe that I might be favorable to moving. Before the annual church meeting, she had spoken to about forty-five men who had been in that church for many decades. I brought the issue of moving to the floor, and they voted overwhelmingly to stay right there. That put that issue to rest.

I then let it be known that we had to start buying buildings. Brown & Williamson had said to me that if there was ever a house or building we wanted and we didn't have the money, Louisville had said they would buy the building on our behalf, hold it until we were ready to buy it, and then sell it to us for the exact price they had paid for it. They never had to do that, however. We raised our own money and purchased twenty-four houses. These were properties directly adjacent to the sanctuary. One of those homes purchased across the alley was the old poolroom. That's where we put our first childcare center. My friend Rev. Andrew White's daughter, Lynn, was our first child at that day care center.

Later, we bought fourteen houses from Raymond Valentine and Churchill Gibson Dunn, who co-owned these properties. Some of them were just shacks with parts of the structure falling in. We paid $12,000 for all fourteen houses. We tore all the houses down and worked on a Saturday morning cleaning up the area. There is a picture in the Heritage Room at Gillfield of us working to get the job done. I remember Granville Robinson cut down one of the trees, and an opossum ran out! We put out bids with various construction companies and Daughtey & Edmonds got the contract. Construction on the building began and was completed in 1969. We had our Christian Education Building!

I have so many wonderful memories from being pastor at Gillfield: sharing life with a host of marvelous people and working to do God's work as hard as I possibly could. Memories of many sermons, weddings, funerals, and meetings fill the recesses of my mind. Gillfield Baptist Church was a wonderful experience for me, a wonderful church with a wonderful congregation indeed.

As the summer of 2012 began, I was working in my garden in the backyard as usual. As the tomato plants grew and I worked to prop them up, I gathered my normal "jerry-rigging" devices such as old stockings and staves of wood to keep bigger stalks from tipping over. As I drove one of those staves in the ground, I had a flashback to when I was out in the field at my daddy's house as a young boy, looking for a stave in the field and calling out to God to help me with certain things going on in my life at the time. I asked God if he wanted me to preach, then let me find that stave and I walked right up on it.

I took pause from my work in the garden and sat down on my upside-down bucket. I just sat there for several minutes and reflected on my relationship with God through the ups and downs of my life. God has been so deeply embedded in my professional calling as a preacher and pastor, but He has also walked with me in the quiet gardens of my life.

In my early years, my approach to God was a simple one: "Lord, if you mean for me to preach, let me find that stave." I wouldn't think of any approach like that today. The God I know is the God that not only serves my simple steps but is also far beyond me. He's so far above me. I used to think of a judgmental God: if I didn't do everything up to snuff, God might hurt me, might come after me. But in my sun setting, I know that there is something about the awesomeness of God that I can never fully explain. But if I try, there is also the grace of God that says, "Grady, you're all right. You've tried and it's ok." It's ok, and I keep going.

So I can look at issues today and see that my biblical interpretation is altogether different than it was in my younger days. Early on, I thought like many others who say that every jot and tittle in the Bible is what God wants us to hear. But it got me in trouble because I began to ask, "How could Jonah stay in the belly of a whale for four days? How did he get the oxygen?" It got me in trouble when I said, "Why did Job suffer so much when he had done nothing wrong? Is the Bible trying to say something else to me that I don't see on the surface?"

And so my life has been one of looking beneath the surface. Some people would say to me, "I wonder if blacks and whites should marry?" I didn't know what to do except what my culture had told me. But I grew to think more about the universality of God. Our God knows people that I don't know. God knows cultures that I don't know. I even grew enough in my life to ask, "What about human kind? Is there human kind that resides on another planet? If so, have they ever known what it means to sin?" I don't know all the answers when I think about the universality of God.

Now, all these things come to my mind; therefore, I have to look beneath the surface in order to analyze things like homosexuality in a different light. I can look at persons who have lost their lives in drugs in a different light. In other words, I have to come to a theology that will fit different kinds of situations. This theology differs from the one I had in my "early afternoon." So the "evening" has been a great time of discovering a broader view of and reflection on God.

There are things that are constant for me: (1) I don't know all about the God that I believe to be God; (2) my lack of knowledge will not destroy my faith; and (3) there are some things that I just accept by faith that I can never prove. For example, I accept and believe in the resurrection of Jesus Christ. I can't prove it, but my faith gives me a kind of personal relationship with him that I can't argue about to others or make them believe. My faith enables me to take what Rudolph Otto calls "a leap of faith," believing what I cannot prove.

He's so far above me. My reflections on God have evolved and have been moving in my life as time has gone "From Morning 'til Evening." The sun is setting, but I still see God walking beside me and talking to me and marching with all of humanity.

The years have continued to move without delay, and the early evening of my life is approaching the still of the night. The normal quietness of the evening for me, however, would still be filled with sermons, weddings, funerals, and meetings.

PART VIII

Sunset and Evening Star

Chapter Fourteen

Thoughts of Sermon Preparation, Life after Retirement, and My Eightieth Birthday

The hour hand of my life approaches sunset. Just like the sunset of any given day, it is a time to wind down daily activities and relax a little. I had been preaching pretty much every Sunday for forty-eight years, and as I began to wind down my activities, I reflected on all those sermons: literally thousands and thousands of sermons. Sometimes, people will ask me about the process of writing and delivering sermons, also known as "homiletics." I used the process of 24/7. Let me explain what I mean.

When I used to drive from Petersburg to Richmond, I always put a tablet down beside me. Any sermon ideas that came to me, I'd write them down. I put a tablet beside my bed and any sermon ideas that came to me in the night, I'd put them down. When I read something in a book, I'd make a note of it if I felt inspiration. I still have quotations in my date book. So that's why I say 24/7.

Then I learned to use a recorder, so that if I was driving, I could just turn it on and start talking. Then in the summer, when I had vacation time, I would develop themes while I was in Pittsburgh visiting Bertie's family. A day here and a day there, and I found it worked well. I would end up with about forty-eight to fifty themes. Then, as a biblical preacher, I would match the theme with biblical passages. I would put all that together and about two weeks in advance, I would have the subject and the text together. I'd say, "This one will be good for the first Sunday; this one will work well for the third Sunday," and so forth.

Then, every Thursday I would take my books and notes with me to the library at Petersburg General Hospital (SRMC). There, in the medical library, I would do most of my sermon writing for Sunday. The librarian, who is living today, was so nice to me. I could leave my books there—Interpreters Bibles and so forth—because she was so happy to be of assistance. When I was at the medical library, the only people who knew where I was were my wife and secretary.

How did I come to retire at sixty-five? Some people thought that was foolish. Some thought I might be sick. Others thought the church had "built a fire under me" and I was in retreat. The real answer was that it was the American Baptist connection and I'll go into detail about that connection in just a moment.

I had a bit of a maverick spirit in me then and now. I've never wanted to walk a well-beaten path. I wanted to make my own path. I think this maverick spirit is apparent in how I was open to women serving in church positions that were usually filled by men. I'm also standing up today for the civil rights of gays. Civil rights and social justice apply to everyone. I'm at the point now where I would consider performing a wedding for gay couples. It's my theology and it's what I believe.

My own mother didn't understand some of my maverick ideologies. For example, when my mother and I were going to take the bus to Aunt Martha's once, I said, "Mama, come on. Let's go and sit on the white side." Mama replied with stern disagreement, "No. Why would we want to do that, Grady?" So there we were, sitting in the bus station, with my mother sitting on the black side and her son sitting on the white side. That was part of my maverick life. What I believed, I wanted to pursue.

So I approached retirement with that same spirit. I had seen so many ministers in my life who came to retirement and couldn't let go. It's a rewarding profession, so I can understand that. Sometimes, though, you have to let go.

One of the pastors who inspired me in my early years just couldn't let go. I will, of course, not mention his name, but he was a towering giant in the work of the church throughout the state of Virginia. He continued to preach as he aged, but when he would get in his car after worship, he sometimes couldn't find his way home. He was getting senile, bless his heart, and he should have retired sooner. With all that said, retirement is still a personal decision.

Often times, however, the main reason a lot of pastors don't want to retire is because they don't have a retirement plan. I had investigated retirement plans when I first came to Petersburg, so I knew at sixty-five years old, I was going to get money and I wouldn't have to be in the rat race. I was getting tired, too, of the heavy schedule I had. Once you start working at a certain level, you can't go back. There was no way I could scale back on what I was doing. There were too many things going on in the city. I was a member of fourteen boards and committees. So why did I retire at sixty-five? No, I wasn't sick. No, the church didn't push me out the door. No, it wasn't that I didn't feel like preaching anymore. I wanted to retire before I was sick, before the church wanted me to leave. I wanted to do some other things that I couldn't do while working as a full-time pastor, like preaching at other places and teaching a little.

My investigation of retirement plans goes back to 1959. I like to call that whole process "The American Baptist Connection." At that time, I went to the Baptist General Convention of Virginia. Interestingly enough, the annual meeting was headquartered at First African Baptist Church on Haynes Avenue in Richmond. The men met at Barton Heights Methodist Church, now known as Garland Avenue Baptist Church, where I currently serve as pastor in residence.

Rev. E. E. Smith of Richmond and Rev. U. G. Wilson of Portsmouth, Virginia, had died. These men were two great leaders of two great churches. The Baptist Allied Bodies, as it was called then, had set up what was called a Ministerial Relief Fund. The rule was that whenever a member pastor died, the fund would give his widow $100, and the members were giving C. L. Evans, the Executive Secretary of the Baptist General Convention, a hard time because Smith and Wilson's widows had not received their $100. Someone raised the issue on the floor, and the members started giving C. L. the third degree. The members were ready to start figuratively breaking chairs over C. L.'s head.

This was my first convention and I asked for the floor. Rev. McCall gave me permission to address the body and I stood to speak. I said, "Mr. President, I'm just joining the Baptist General Convention and I want to plead with you that if I die, please do not give my widow $100. I love that lady too much for you to give her $100, because if that's all she has, I'd rather you shoot her summarily. If you give her $100, it's like cutting off her toe first, and then half a foot, then the whole foot, and it might take three or four days for her to die. I'd rather you just shoot her." That got everyone's attention, and they just laughed. I mean, what's a widow going to do with $100? That's nothing. I continued by saying, "Therefore, I believe we need a retirement plan." Bob Taylor, who was buried in 2012, got right up after I finished my statement and said, "I hope we will be the last pastors that have no retirement."

Cary S. McCall appointed a committee to look into my suggestion of a retirement plan. He named me chairman of the committee. I was twenty-seven years old. On the committee with me were Bob Taylor, Y. B. Williams, and Tom Venable. I wrote a letter to New York Life Insurance, Prudential, and others. I also wrote to various religious organizations, including American Baptist.

One day when I was at Quioccasin, someone knocked on my door. I opened the door and a man said, "Rev. Powell, I'm Martin England with American Baptist and we received your letter about a retirement plan." He explained to me that American Baptist had a retirement plan that might work for us. Their retirement plan had been set up by John D. Rockefeller, Sr., who had been a member of Riverside Church, an American Baptist Church in New York, because he had felt his pastor should have a retirement plan. That was in 1903.

Mr. England said, "We would like for you to visit us in Valley Forge, Pennsylvania." Wow! I was elated. To understand the desire of American Baptist, one needs to reference 1845. The Southern Baptists and Northern Baptists split. The Northern Baptists couldn't get a foothold in the South, so building a relationship with the Baptist General Convention of Virginia was very attractive to them. We were 300 churches strong.

We rode to Valley Forge in Bob Taylor's Lincoln. They gave us the royal treatment. Every American Baptist department attended the meetings, and they entertained us for two days. They put us in a hotel and paid for it. Martin England said that any church that wanted to join the American Baptist retirement plan immediately would have one year to build it into their budget, during which time American Baptist would pay for the plan for them. That's how I got into American Baptist. Gillfield was the third church in Virginia to join. So once a month now, I receive a direct deposit right into my checking account due to those early years of planning things out and preparing for the future I knew would come.

Joining American Baptist was like being part of royalty. I got on the Board of Education, which put me on the General Board. That was an education within itself. I saw denominational work being done like I had never seen in my life. They had hundreds of thousands of dollars that they used to send missionaries around the globe. They had programs in urban areas designed to help those in need. In Green Lake, Wisconsin, they had a retreat center for pastors, to which I was able to take my whole family. It was nestled amongst hills, valleys, and lakes. It was beautiful! They had the M & M Board for retirement plans in New York. I became a member of the Ecumenical Commission, which put me on the National Council of Churches of Christ. I went to the 7th Assembly of the World Council of Churches in British Columbia. I was connected to national organizations and boards that were connected to political statements that came out of the White House. The American Baptist connection was truly "God sent."

During my final months as pastor of Gillfield, I even took a few side jobs in an effort to prepare myself for life after retirement. One such endeavor was with a local Petersburg company called Diversity Foods, where I served as the industrial chaplain on my day off, which was Tuesday. I went to the deacon board at Gillfield and told them about it. I told them I wanted to start this and it was going to be part of my retirement. They said they thought that would be wonderful and supported me wholeheartedly.

In February of 1997, I decided that I wanted to announce my retirement. I had started preaching when I was seventeen, so I had been preaching pretty much every Sunday for forty-eight years. My announcement came eight months before it would actually occur, and on the Saturday before the fourth Sunday in February, I wrote my statement. I was in the dining room, a place I often used to write sermons. Some moments last forever, and I'll never forget that day and that moment. After I wrote it, I called my wife into the room. She is someone who has stood so closely by me through it all. She didn't know anything about it. I said, "Bertie, I want to read you something." I started reading my retirement statement to her and I broke down crying right there in front of her. She came over and put her arms around me and said, "Oh, Grady! It's going to be all right . . . it's going to be all right!" But I finished reading it to her. Crying or not, I was going to retire.

Retirement is a very emotional thing, particularly when your whole life has been given to your career. Many of the people I worked with at Gillfield Baptist Church had been with me for thirty-seven years. I baptized people and then baptized their children. I dedicated babies and married couples while burying others. I am also pleased to say that due to the cooperation of Pastor Bill Higgins and Rev. Keith Savage, both of Manassas, I was able to baptize both my grandsons: Grady Powell III and Harvey "Champ" Woodson. It's all been very emotional.

Between February and November of 1997, I had all kinds of doubts about my decision. I would think, "You didn't mean that . . . you shouldn't have done that." Many of my preacher friends thought something was wrong and would ask me, "Why are you retiring now?" I stuck with my decision and decided I was going to preach my last sermon on the first Sunday in November, because it would occur right after the church's 200th anniversary celebration.

I had gotten John Sunquist to preach as the final speaker during our bicentennial ceremonies. We celebrated our bicentennial for fourteen months. I had booked him a year in advance. John was a big deal because he served as the Executive Minister of International Ministries for the American Baptist Church USA. The plan was to get him to speak on the fourth Sunday in October 1997. The following Sunday would be my final sermon.

That day came as surely as the hands of time keep moving. What was I to preach about? My final sermon was about the constancy of God. What I tried to emphasize was this: the Lord has been our dwelling place in all generations. I was trying to say that God was at Gillfield before I got there. I was convinced God was at Gillfield while I was there, and that he would remain at Gillfield after I was gone. I charged, go with God, and continue to regularly read your Bible.

I decided that on that Sunday I would cut off all physical connections with Gillfield Church because I knew I loved them so much. It would be hard to give them up. It was hard. I remember that Dr. Earl Allgood would be the church administrator and that he would come into the office according to his schedule. Earl had decided that he would not take any salary but committed to come at least two days a week. He had worked his professional life teaching statistics at Virginia State University and he loved Gillfield so much. He was dedicated to the progress of Gillfield and was one of the highest givers financially in the church.

I told Earl I was going to give him the keys to the church that day, and I did. In my office, I said a prayer with him, praying for us both, and I walked out of Gillfield Baptist Church for the last time as pastor. I did not go back inside that church for three months.

It goes without saying that upon my announcement of retirement, I asked myself, "What am I going to do?" The *Progress-Index*, the local Petersburg newspaper, interviewed me about my retirement from Gillfield. The article was entitled "A Journey of Faith." I talked about the life I anticipated after retirement and said that any train that was going someplace, I would reach for, grab onto, and ride, because I was afraid that I would be bored.

When people would call me and say, "We want you to preach," I would take it. I started collecting preaching engagements. Dr. Allix B. James, my teacher and mentor and former president of Virginia Union, called me and said, "Grady, I'm going on a trip to Africa. Would you teach a class for me?" My quick response was "I'd be glad to!" He wanted me to start in thirty days. American Baptist, division of clergy, said one of the things I could do was take the job of preaching at various churches around the country. They would arrange the dates, and I could be in Massachusetts, Arizona, California, or so forth. John Sunquist told me that he wished I would take a few engagements in Cincinnati first. He said he would mention my name. The church officials wanted to try a black preacher, he explained. I thought that would be interesting, preaching to a white congregation. I did it and wasn't there for three weeks before I realized that it was too much: flying out Saturday morning and flying back Tuesday morning, and by the time I would settle into being home for a few days, it was time to think about flying back.

Well, my fear of boredom had led me into a reality of being overbooked. I had to give up a few things. It was obvious to me that I needed single tasks that I could concentrate on. Then I was asked to be the interim pastor at Mount Olive Baptist Church in Richmond, Virginia. Cessar Scott, Executive Director of the Baptist General Convention, talked about that and I agreed to do it and I liked it. The people of Mount Olive embraced me and I embraced them. Next I went to Fourth Baptist in the same capacity for three years, then to St. James Church in Varina. The next stop was at Morning Star Baptist Church. I went from there to Westwood Baptist Church, and now I'm at Garland Avenue Baptist Church, also in Richmond. I've done interim pastorates at six different churches in the Richmond area and I've enjoyed every minute of it. I've met so many wonderful people who just want to praise God like I do.

Fortunately for me, the current Pastor of Gillfield, Rev. Dr. George W. C. Lyons, is a wonderful friend. Although he is much younger than I, we have a close relationship. He often reaches out to show a caring spirit, and for this I am grateful.

One Gillfield couple sent me a card with their personal expressions after Rev. Lyons held a Pastor Emeritus Appreciation Day for me. It reads as follows:

Dear Rev. Grady Wilson Powell,

We are sorry we could not be at church on the Sunday they celebrated you as Pastor Emeritus. Now we want to take this opportunity to show our appreciation for the light you brought into our lives.

It is with honor and great joy that we say 'thank you.' You have a gift of encouraging others and making them feel as though they are the most important person in the room. Thank you for your spiritual leadership and guidance. We benefited greatly from your warm and jubilant personality, pleasing disposition, diplomacy and encouragement. You gave so much of yourself with grace and a servant's heart.

Now it's our time to give a little back. Your name continues to be a source of joy around our house. Thank you again for being such a blessing to us. We love you and we pray God's continual blessings on you, Mrs. Powell, and your family.

Dave, Sharon, David, & Tedra Embry

Another memorable experience has been with a family who was not a member of any church I served as pastor or interim pastor. My contact with this family came through a member of the church I served as pastor-in-residence. The following is a direct excerpt from the letter I received after a funeral:

Thank you . . . for entering my family's life at my mother's funeral. I cannot thank you enough for entering in as only God could have sent you.

You were the perfect Pastor, the perfect man, and the perfect soul to stand there and share the most comforting words . . . , especially to me, the baby.

We all had a tremendous loss . . . , but I lost so much more as we were living together for years after the passing of our father. She was my very best friend, my buddy, my roommate, my partner, my patient near the end, and my everything in ALL things; my mother simply was my world . . .

Our kindest thoughts will remain for you and your family forever, and our appreciation for what you did for us will never be forgotten throughout my entire family . . . Your name has truly become beloved with our family.

There are times when God walks through your life and never leaves an imprint but you know he's there. And through you Rev. Powell, God told me to remember my mother is with Him and to rejoice . . . and find the best memories and happiness.

Love to you, Rev. Powell and your family . . . All good things are wished for you and yours.

Debra Coleman and the Thornton Family

The interim pastorates have meant a lot to me. One reason I appreciate them is that I enjoy preaching and I have to preach. But I decided I didn't want to preach every Sunday. I really would have preferred preaching twice a month. Another benefit of the interim pastorates was I have many manuscripts, so I don't have to research as I did in the original writing of the sermon. The third benefit that has come from these interim pastorates is that my circle of close friends has expanded tremendously. I could stand and name to you a hundred very close friends who have come out of these interim pastorates. It has also been extra income, but not as much as some people think.

I have also been able in these interim pastorates to take my experiences and see what works and what doesn't work; when to tread softly and when to carry a big stick. There are so many different styles of worship, some of which don't fit me well, but I have learned what Paul said: "In whatever state I am therewith to be content." I have learned, as Paul, how to be satisfied with little or much. Life after the pastorate has been wonderful! It has been a time when I don't have to concentrate as much on the daily operations of the church. I can concentrate on the greater meaning of the church spiritually. I have to get involved with some administration and of course I do get involved with some counseling. However, I am greatly involved in spirituality and representing the church.

As I look up at the sun and see it shining over my life, and my years have passed midday, I can see it is going down. It is not as hot as it was at midday and the big chores of my life have somewhat declined. There is the warmth as the breeze comes from the south and I reflect back on days gone by. There is also sometimes a chilled wind from the north, but I have found out that I can get along well and be very happy in retirement. I can serve as much as I want and when I get ready to relinquish a task, I can just say to the man who operates the train, "I'm getting off, sir." I have learned this: that when life is difficult or easy, when it is sad or joyful, when it's long or short, I know whate'er befalls me, Jesus doeth all things well.

As this life narrative comes to a conclusion, I have come to my eightieth birthday. I trust my sunset will be an extended one. From my morning 'til evening, I see shadows that have gathered with some sobering yet joyful messages.

At this birthday, there are many persons who have made my eightieth year more than special. I have appreciated the showers of love from the pastor of Gillfield and his wife, Dr. and Mrs. George W. C. Lyons, the congregation of Gillfield, and Garland Avenue Baptist Church, where I currently serve as pastor in residence. I have also appreciated the statements of my wife and children that they shared with me through cards and letters. I share them as lasting mementos of my life.

From my wife:

After fifty-nine years of marriage, I remain convinced that God sent me from Pittsburgh, Pennsylvania, to Virginia—not just to attend a college—but to meet, love, and cherish you, to give birth and rear our five precious children, and to share our lives together until time, by death, separates us.

The following words from my greeting card to you on your 80th birthday further express the ties that bind us:

Yours is the smile I look forward to each morning, and yours is the voice I love to hear throughout the day . . .

Yours are the plans and dreams that blend with mine, and yours is the love that means the world to me.

My life would be so different if you weren't a part of it, and that is why no one has more to celebrate today than I do . . .

To my husband, my soul mate, my very best friend . . .

From Sandra:

In your 80 years, Dad, you have given me those gifts all fathers should give: shelter, food, and resources to make a viable independent and healthy life. Yet you have given me far more: (1) A real thirst for knowledge—the purpose in "knowing" was not just to know but to use that knowledge for a greater good. (2) A work ethic—to be able to provide for oneself and "do good work" is a gift. More important is that whatever the work, you taught me that what I promise, I should do, and do it well. (3) An ability to laugh from the gut and to see the lighter side of all things. And most important, (4) a consistent reminder that "God is" . . . no matter what, there is still God. I could not have had a more dedicated and loving father.

From Dot:

While it is your birthday, I feel like I am the one who should celebrate. I feel like celebrating because God has given me a great person to be my father. Over the years, you have shown me and my siblings love, kindness, forgiveness, generosity, and most importantly, godliness. You have been and continue to be a living example of a good man in a troubled world. I know that your life has not been easy, but through your hard work, loving care, and spirituality, you have made my life—both as a child and as an adult—a lot easier. And for these reasons, I will always love and honor you—now and for all of my living days. I love you, Dad.

From Grady Jr.:

Each day and every moment of life is so precious, and so today, we are so excited to share with you the joy of your 80th birthday. We are grateful to God for giving you the gift of long life. You still have a strong mind and good health and we pray that God will continue to bless you as you carry on your mission . . . a spiritual mission that has extended itself far beyond our family.

You're just a great guy and I feel so fortunate to be your son, your friend, and your student. Continue to walk this life with the dignity of a new crown . . . the crown of 80 years. I love you always.

From Herb:

As we celebrate your 80th birthday, there isn't a better time to simply say how much I love and respect you. I told a friend of mine recently that from the time I was a boy, I have never left your presence without my self-esteem intact. In times of correction and in times of encouragement, you always dealt with me with a gentle strength; and I am so grateful to you for that.

I am also grateful for your priceless humor, which has been and continues to be what made our house a home. Those jovial seeds continue to flower in the homes of your children and in the lives your children touch.

I'm most in debt for the very personal choices you've made as a man. I suspect it was something you picked up from your parents in the wide-open spaces of southeast Virginia that contributed to your desire to make a mark on the souls that would come across your doorstep. Your parents were and are proud of you.

Since life is the beautiful and challenging journey that it is, I'm so thankful to God that he graced my life with a father just like you.

From Eric:

There are so many things I appreciate about you, Dad, but one of them stands out, mainly because it has been the greatest tool of my adult life.

You are a man of conviction and strong beliefs, but the doors of conversation, curiosity, and challenging one's own belief system are never closed. There was never a time I thought I couldn't talk to you about anything. As a teenager, I had things that I may have felt timid (or embarrassed) about, but I never felt talking to you was off limits. You were always able to give the human touch and point out the broader picture of situations. Even if sharing my thoughts went against your own belief system, you taught me never to be afraid to think. I am so happy that you are my Dad.

As I continue to walk this life, I often reflect back on the early morning period of time. Those events scatter through my memory like the wind as it blows through the trees. Sometimes as I walk to my garden at my home in Petersburg, I can envision those early years when I would walk to the fields on the farm with Daddy and my siblings. As I pick up the grubbing hoe, shovel, and whatnot in my own backyard, I can see Daddy's hands doing the same thing, way back when, down in the fields of Brunswick County.

My life has come full circle. In this "late evening" period, I'm right back where I started—not just in the gardens with dirt, but also in the gardens of life, where I still experience the joy of family with Bertie, my children, my grandsons, sons-in-law, and daughter-in-law. We are a close family. We abide in love and the joy of one another, just as I did with Daddy, Mama, Buster, Mable, Pert, Mert, Toot, and Irene. My family, from which I came, has gone now, but the Lord my God has continued to bless me with family. I have nieces and nephews, a congregation to serve, and a host of friends and neighbors with whom I can interact and whom I cherish, each and every one of them.

I've lived for the love of God, who has blessed me with long life. I've walked this life with as much courage and dignity as I could muster. In every opportunity that I could, I did my best to reach out my hand and help someone in need so that my living would not be in vain, and from the pulpit I continue to share the good news of Jesus Christ our Lord.

The music of life and living has been a wonderful song for me. I continue daily to sing that song of life as I carry on. Sometimes life's melody may be sad and sometimes joyous, but I continue to sing . . .

I walk with the King, Hallelujah
I walk with the King, praise his name . . .
From Morning 'til Evening
Glad tidings I sing
I walk and I talk with the King.

ABOUT THE AUTHOR

Grady Wilson Powell, a native of Brunswick County, Virginia, has had a varied career in education and the professional ministry. He attended a one-room elementary school and an episcopal high school located on a college campus. He holds a bachelor of science degree from St. Paul's College (1954), a master of divinity degree from Virginia Union University (1959), a doctor of divinity degree from St. Paul's College (1976), and a doctor of humane letters degree from Virginia Union University (2012). He has done further study at Union Theological Seminary in Richmond, Virginia.

Along with a brief teaching career, he has served four rural churches; however, his heart's desire was to be a full-time pastor, and that occurred for him in 1958 when he became pastor of Quioccasin Baptist Church in Richmond, Virginia, and then pastor of Gillfield Baptist Church in Petersburg, Virginia, for thirty-six years.

Dr. Powell's outreach beyond Gillfield has been extensive. He has served on many boards and committees and has been honored on several occasions. After his retirement, he assisted six churches as interim pastor and continued to share his life in community service.

He is married to Dr. Bertie J. Powell, a retired professor of English from Virginia State University. They have five children (Sandra, Dorthula, Grady Jr., Herbert, and Eric) and two grandchildren (Harvey III and Grady III).